FASCINATING

OBJECT LESSONS

FASCINATING
OBJECT LESSONS

By
ARNOLD CARL WESTPHAL

BAKER BOOK HOUSE
Grand Rapids, Michigan

Formerly published under the title,
Junior Surprise Sermons
© 1934 by Fleming H. Revell Co.
Paperback edition issued 1977
by Baker Book House
ISBN: 0-8010-9594-8

PHOTOLITHOPRINTED BY CUSHING - MALLOY, INC.
ANN ARBOR, MICHIGAN, UNITED STATES OF AMERICA
1977

PREFACE

THE purpose of this volume is to fill a long felt need, expressed by thousands of workers with children.

Organization and publication of material began a number of years ago, during a busy pastorate in the city of Chicago, where hundreds of children could be gathered from the streets in a few moments. Four groups of children were "discovered."

1. Those who were all MOUTH. For these, singing proved helpful.
2. Those who were all EARS. A story-teller could interest these.
3. Those who were all HANDS AND FEET. Games were provided for this group.
4. Those who were all EYES. Truly the "Eyes" had it, for they far outnumbered the others.

It was found that dullness and inattention, mischief and wrangling, waxing boldness and waning interest were lost, when "All eyes were to the front." This discovery prompted the author's specialization in VISUAL TEACHING, with the consequent creations that have been and are being passed on to others with similar problems.

Under persuasion, organized material was put into marketable form, for general circulation. This resulted in the naming and manufacturing of what is now on the market as *Twenty-five Visual Evangels (Series Number 1)*.

Hundreds of interested Pastors, Sunday School Teachers, Missionaries, Superintendents, Summer Bible School Leaders, Children's Evangelists and Workers in general have used these. Popular request then led to the creation and marketing of a second group of Visual Sermons, known as *Twenty-five Visual Evangels (Series Number 2)*. These have found their way into every part of the land, and across the seas, and in every denomination, until circulation has run into many thousands. Since then, other such series have been added, the latest being named *Visual Evangelettes*.

The author now desires to submit an entirely new group of Visual Sermons, like unto the others, except that the object, or centre of Visual

Interest is to be built by the workers, instead of being supplied, ready-made by the author. Hence the many drawings and plans in the book.

The author has kept in mind, simplicity, in the making of the object with material that is easily found, such as paper, cardboard, glue, crayon, paints, etc. He has put each lesson through a series of experiments on children of all ages, in Sunday School, Week-Day Bible School, Summer or Vacation Bible Schools, Saturday Afternoon Children's Bible Chautauqua, Sunday Morning Worship, Junior Church, Young People's Societies, and before the noon-day "soup" gatherings of hundreds of under-nourished children. They have proven out equally successful, under all circumstances where children gather.

The author has kept in mind the one element that makes these sermons different from the average sermon for children—that is, the "Surprise" element. The "Surprise" climax captivates the attention of the children under the most extreme conditions, and clinches the truth, and brings them curiously near "the man of God" for further enlightenment.

In addition to these tests, the sermons have been presented, as a method, before student bodies of Training Bible Schools, Assemblies, Institutes, Conventions, Leadership Training Schools, Pastors' Retreats, Ministerial Associations, etc. In each case they have been favourably received, with commendation, because of their obvious logic, simplicity, evangelistic appeal, character building quality and grip of the heart through the eye.

That this book might prove a manual of visual helpfulness and instruction, to the ever increasing host of Children's Workers who yearn for God's Little Lambs, these pages are prayerfully surrendered to "the eyes of the world."

A. C. W.

Salem, Ohio.

CONTENTS

10

FASCINATING
OBJECT LESSONS

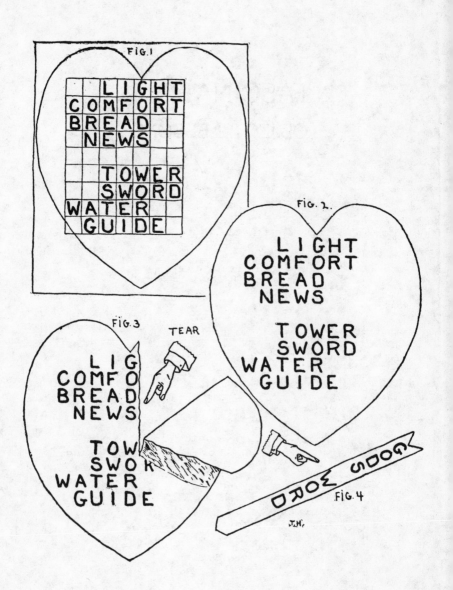

FIG. 1

LIGHT
COMFORT
BREAD
NEWS

TOWER
SWORD
WATER
GUIDE

FIG. 2.

LIGHT
COMFORT
BREAD
NEWS

TOWER
SWORD
WATER
GUIDE

FIG. 3

TEAR

LIG OD
COMF O
BREAD
NEWS

TOW
SWOR
WATER
GUIDE

FIG. 4

J.H.

I

THE HIDDEN HEART TREASURE *

(Suitable for Bible School or Worship Services on Universal Bible Sunday)

MATERIAL NEEDED—

White wrapping paper.
Crayon or paint.
Scissors.
A Bible.

CONSTRUCTION OF OBJECT—

1. Print words of Fig. 1 on the wrapping paper, in proper order, with "GOD'S WORD" down the centre. Pencil mark squares will help you make proportionate letters. Erase squares later.

2. Draw a large heart around lettering, and cut into shape.

THE LESSON

Boys and girls, there is a Hidden Treasure in this heart. Watch carefully, for I will take it out and show it to you a little later.

The Psalmist said

"Thy word have I hid in my heart, that I might not sin against thee," Psalm 119:11.

THREE GREAT WONDERS

He had a WONDERFUL thing: "Thy word."
In a WONDERFUL place: "In my heart."
For a WONDERFUL purpose: "That I might not sin."

A LIGHT TO MY PATH

1. The same treasure hidden in this heart, is also hidden in my heart, and I hope you will hide it in yours, too.

---

* Published first in *Church Management*. Later, in the Free Methodist, *Sunday School Worker*.

That treasure is a LIGHT to my path. (Point to LIGHT.)

Some time ago, men were digging in the Bible lands. We call these men "Archæologists," and they dig up many things that prove the Bible is true. They are great scholars, but their main tools are a pick and shovel.

These men, one day, found a number of funny-looking little lamps. Each lamp had two small rings and one large ring. They also found some stone slabs with writing on them, and the writing mentioned "Foot-Lamps." One of these men took off his shoe to see if he could fit this lamp on his foot. He discovered that the big ring was for his big toe, and the other two rings were for straps to go through to hold the lamp in place.

The people often went barefooted or wore soft sandals, and at night it was important that they see where they stepped, so they had these foot-lamps to light their path. This is what the Psalmist had in mind when he said, "Thy Word is a lamp unto my feet and a light unto my path."

A GREAT COMFORT

2. The Hidden Treasure in my heart is also a great COMFORT. Many times I am called upon to stand before a death-bed or casket or open grave, to speak words of comfort to people in sorrow. My own words fail me, so I always carry this hidden treasure with me, for it can give great comfort. (Hold up the Bible.) It has over thirty thousand promises in it, and every one will be fulfilled. One of its greatest promises is this, "If ye abide in Me, and My words abide in you, ye shall ask what ye will and it shall be done unto you" (John 15:7).

BREAD TO A HUNGRY SOUL

3. This Hidden Treasure is also BREAD to my hungry soul. It satisfied the hungry Jesus, too. When Satan told Jesus to turn the stones into bread, Jesus said, "Man shall not live by bread alone, but by every word that proceedeth out of the mouth of God" (Matt. 4:4).

Jeremiah said, "Thy words were found, and I did eat them, and Thy word was unto me the joy and rejoicing of my heart" (chap. 15:16).

Many have this treasure lying on the shelf, but unless we hide it in our hearts it will do us no good. Only as we eat are we fed.

A man said, "I have been through the Bible five times now, and I feel no closer to God than I did." A friend said to him, "You may have gone through the Bible five times, but how many times has the Bible gone through you?"

If this treasure is to be bread to my soul, it must be hidden in my heart.

GOOD NEWS TO MY SOUL

4. The Hidden Treasure is good NEWS to my soul. It covers the past, present and future. It tells me that Jesus died for my sins in the past. It tells me that Jesus keeps me day by day, in the present, and it tells me that He will call me home to Himself, to the House of Many Mansions, in the future. What great, good news this is!

A BEACON-TOWER

5. The Hidden Treasure in my heart is also like a TOWER. It is like the great Beacon Light Towers that guide the lonely aeroplane pilots at night, over the great airways. Without these towers, they would be lost in the night. *Also like Lighthouses*

A SHARP SWORD

6. This Hidden Treasure is also like a SWORD that protects me. Paul said to the Ephesians, "Take the helmet of salvation, and the sword of the Spirit, which is the word of God" (Ephesians 6:17).

The Book of Hebrews says, "The word of God is quick and powerful and sharper than any two-edged sword" (chap. 4:12).

With this sword, Jesus drove the tempter away. Three times Jesus said, "It is written." Each time He quoted a part of God's word, and then the devil left Him and angels came and ministered unto Him.

WATER TO MY THIRSTY SOUL

7. This Hidden Treasure is like refreshing WATER to my thirsty soul. It is like a great bubbling fountain of life.

DYING FOR WATER

A man was lost in the desert, dying for lack of water. A drink could save his life. Suddenly he saw a water-can lying in the sand. He fell down upon it and opened it, like a mad man. He put it to his mouth for a drink, but, to his great disappointment, it had only diamonds in it. Precious as diamonds are, he could not drink those, and he died.

This Hidden Treasure in my heart waters my thirsty soul, even in desert places.

A CONSTANT GUIDE

8. The Hidden Treasure is also a GUIDE for my life. A guide is like a railroad timetable. It tells me where to go, and how to get there.

REVIEW

9. Let us review, and then I will keep my promise, and show you the Hidden Treasure in this heart.

The Hidden Treasure is:

A LIGHT to my path;

A COMFORT in the time of trouble;

BREAD to my hungry soul;

GOOD NEWS to my sinful heart;

A TOWER to guide me in my wandering ways;

A SWORD in my hand;

WATER to my thirsty soul;

A GUIDE to my weary footsteps.

And here is the Hidden Treasure right in the very centre of the heart, just where it belongs. (Cut out the centre of heart, from top to bottom.)

GOD'S WORD

This is the Hidden Treasure the Psalmist said we should hide in our hearts, lest we sin against God.

ADDITIONAL ILLUSTRATIONS

To many people, the Bible is just another book, to be placed on the library table or on the shelf behind the door. God said we should hide it—but not behind the door. It should be hidden in the heart.

MOTH BALLS IN THE CLOTHES BOX

We put moth balls in the clothes box to keep out the moths, lest they eat holes in the clothing.

If we protect a fifteen-dollar coat that will be worn out in three years, don't you think we should protect our souls from the moths of sin?

The soul is more precious than all the world and it doesn't wear out in three years, but will last throughout eternity. Therefore, protect it by hiding the moth balls of God's Word in your heart.

You can't improve the product, but the product can improve the container in which it is kept, if the product is God's Word, and the container is the heart.

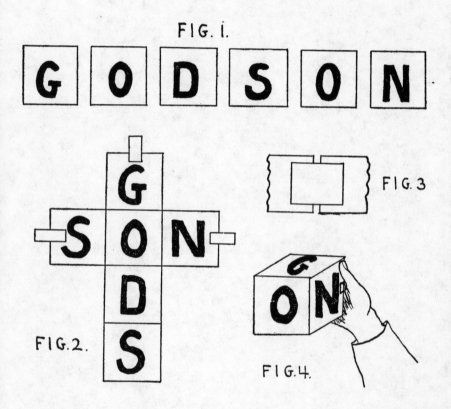

FIG. 1.

FIG. 2.

FIG. 3

FIG. 4.

II

GOD'S GREAT GIFT-BOX *

(Suitable for any Sunday—but especially good for Christmas)

MATERIAL NEEDED—

Cardboard.
Paper and glue or sealing tape.
Crayon or paint.

CONSTRUCTION OF OBJECT—

1. Cut six pieces of cardboard, 4 x 4 inches. Fig. 1.
2. Lay squares in form of cross. Fig. 2.
3. Hinge together with paper and glue. Fig. 3.
4. Print letters on face side of cross. Fig. 2.
5. Paste small labels on squares G and S and N. Fig. 2.
6. Fold cross into shape of square box, and seal to hold shape. Fig. 4.

THE LESSON

I have in my hand a Gift-Box. In it is the greatest gift ever given to the world. Watch this box, and listen carefully, and later I will open the box to let you see what is in it, and then you will see the greatest gift that was ever given to the world.

IT WAS A GIFT FROM GOD

Most of you have received gifts in boxes, and how anxious you are to see what is inside. The Wise Men, when they came to worship Jesus, the new-born King, brought gifts. I often wondered if they brought the gifts of gold, frankincense and myrrh in little boxes.

You have had birthday and Christmas gifts, and when you finish school, someone might give you a graduation gift. On Mother's Day we get Mother a gift, and on Father's Day, we get Father one.

God in heaven looked down upon His children on earth, and saw their sorrow, brought on by sin. He saw their happiness marred, and only

---

* First published in *Church Management.*

19

death to look forward to. He had a gift which, if He gave and people would accept, would change their sorrow to happiness, and their sin to salvation, and their death to life; so, at a very great sacrifice, He sent them the gift that is in this box.

THE MYSTERIOUS LETTERS ON THE GIFT-BOX

Before opening a gift-box, we always read what is on the outside, to try to find out from whom it came. Sometimes we can tell what is in the box by reading what is on the outside.

Let us see if we can get a hint at what is in this wonderful box. I see here the letter G. It might stand for gold. Some think that gold is the greatest gift, but it is not. God's great gift was not gold.

IT WAS NOT SILVER

I also see the letter S. That may stand for silver, but that is not the greatest gift either, for the Bible says, "What shall it profit a man if he gain the whole world, and lose his own soul?"

IT WAS NOT DIAMONDS

Here is the letter D. Could that stand for diamonds? Is that the greatest gift? No. Precious stones could bring happiness, but not salvation, and that was what we needed when God sent His gift.

IT WAS NOT OTHER JEWELS

Here is another letter S. That stands for sapphires. They are beautiful and expensive, but could not give us salvation. Here is the letter O. That could stand for onyx or opal, yet neither of these are the great gift from God.

IT WAS NOT A GREAT NAME

I see here the letter N. That stands for name. Some think if they had a great name and became famous, that would be the greatest gift. That was not the gift that God sent.

WE MUST OPEN THE BOX

What was the gift? We will have to open the box to see. (Tear the small labels that hold the box in shape.)

Well, it is not a box now, at all, is it? It is a cross, and the gift is—let us spell it out—G-O-D-'s S-O-N. (Point to these letters as you spell them out.) That spells GOD's SON.

Of course, this was the greatest gift God could give. It was the gift of His love, and it cost Him more than any other gift, for it was His Own Son that He gave. "For God so loved the world that He gave His only begotten Son, that whosoever believeth in Him should not perish, but have everlasting life" (John 3:16).

ILLUSTRATIVE MATERIAL

The late D. L. Moody used to tell about the prairie fires in the West. When a fire was seen to be coming, people started a fire on the spot where they were standing, and burned the grass down around them. Then when the fire approached this spot, it would die out, for there was nothing to burn there, and the people were saved. So God also gave us a place of refuge. It is at the Cross of Calvary. It is like water in the wilderness or desert.

> *"Beneath the cross of Jesus*
> *I fain would take my stand,*
> *The shadow of a mighty rock*
> *Within a weary land;*
> *A home within the wilderness,*
> *A rest upon the way,*
> *From the burning of the noon-tide heat,*
> *And the burden of the day."*

THE ONLY SON OF A MOTHER

A mother had an only son. He was converted, and was later called upon to go to Africa as a missionary. As he went, the mother said, "I never knew before how much it cost God to give us His only Son as a gift.

FURTHER VISUALIZATION

Various colours of paper, pasted on the squares, would help. Yellow for gold, silver for silver, etc. This would visualize more surely for the children.

22

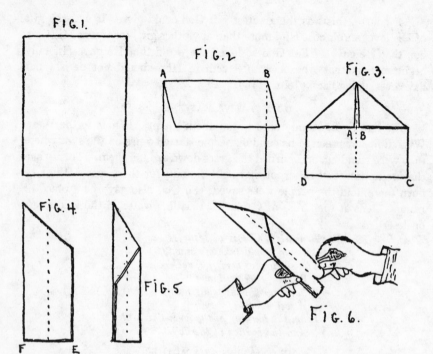

FIG. 1.

FIG. 2.

A   B

FIG. 3.

A B

D   C

FIG. 4.

FIG. 5.

F   E

FIG. 6.

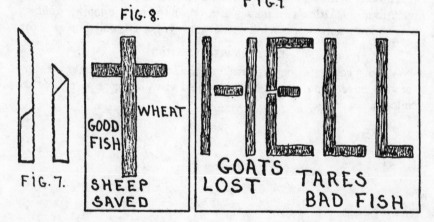

FIG. 9.

FIG. 8.

FIG. 7.

GOOD FISH

WHEAT

SHEEP SAVED

HELL

GOATS LOST   TARES BAD FISH

III

TWO ROADS TO ETERNITY

"There is a way that seemeth right unto a man, but the end thereof are the ways of death."—PROVERBS 14:12.

"Wide is the gate and broad is the way that leadeth to destruction, and many there be that go in thereat, because strait is the gate, and narrow is the way which leadeth unto life, and few there be that find it."—MATTHEW 7:13-14.

MATERIAL NEEDED—

Gummed paper.
Cardboard.
Two common pins.
Scissors.
Crayon or paint.

CONSTRUCTION OF OBJECT—

1. Get two pieces of coloured cardboard. Figs. 8 and 9. Fig. 8 should be 9 x 12 inches.

2. Get a piece of white gummed paper, 7 x 11 inches. Fig. 1.

3. Fold Fig. 1, as in Fig. 2, keeping the gummed side toward you. Fold corners A and B down, as in Fig. 3. Fold Fig. 3 lengthwise, down middle. Fig. 4. Fold Fig. 4 lengthwise down middle as in Fig 5. Tear Fig. 5 down the middle (during the lesson, as in Fig. 6, forming the two parts of Fig. 7.

These parts, when unfolded, should make a cross, and the small parts will spell HELL.

4. As you develop the lesson, before the children, parts should be pasted on the card. All can be pasted on gummed side except last L. Pin this to board.

IMPORTANT NOTE

It is strongly advocated that you go before the children with the unfolded paper. Then fold it as you talk. This will greatly add to the effect.

THE LESSON

Today, boys and girls, I want to point to the great future. The Bible calls it Eternity. Eternity is what comes after we die. Some of you may live to be ninety, but others might die while still very young.

THE GIRL WHO MEASURED THE GRAVES

Once a small girl asked her mother how big one had to be before he died. The wise mother told her to go to the cemetery, and with a piece of string, to measure the length of the graves, and for each different length, to tie a knot in the string. This she did, and she had knots all over the string, for she found graves, long and short. Then she understood that even children are big enough to die.

THE SUBJECT: TWO ROADS TO ETERNITY

Our subject reminds us that life is made up of two's. We have light and dark, good and bad, hard and soft, large and small, black and white, slow and fast, high and low, up and down, over and under, in and out, sickness and health, life and death, and we have HEAVEN and HELL.

Jesus teaches us that there is a right and wrong road. He said one road was broad, and the other narrow. The broad road is the easy road, but it is the road of sin, and many choose it. The end is very sad.

The other road is narrow and hard, and only the courageous few choose it. This is the road of the Christian. Though hard and bumpy, the end is very happy.

HEAVEN AND HELL

Jesus called the ends of these two roads heaven and hell. Heaven is where the Christians go after death, for they travel the narrow road, but hell is where the lost go, who travel the broad road, the road of disobedience.

THE PAPER-FOLD

I want to fold this paper, and a little later I will tear it up into two parts, and each of the two parts will stand for one of the roads.

(Fold paper as instructed, so it will be ready to be torn, as in Fig. 6.)

THE WHEAT AND THE TARES

Jesus always warned people about the wrong road. He said that once a man sowed some good seed in his field. Then one night, when he slept, an enemy came and sowed weeds or tares in his field. Both the wheat and the tares grew together until harvest time. Then the wheat was separated from the tares. The wheat was put into the barn, but the tares were burned.

The wheat represents the good people, and the tares represent the lost.

Both will live together until the end of life, and then in the harvest, the Christians will go to heaven, and the lost will go to hell. Matt. 13:24-30.

THE GOOD AND BAD FISH

Jesus also said these two roads were like a fisherman with a great drag-net. The net was dragged in the sea, and all kinds of fish were caught. At the end of the day, the fisherman sorted the fish, keeping the good fish, and throwing out the bad fish. Then Jesus said that in the end of the world the angels will separate the good people who are Christians from the bad people (Matt. 13:47-50).

FURTHER THOUGHTS

(This thought can be carried out further if desired, using such passages as The Two Ways (Psalm 1), The Wise and Foolish Virgins, The Sheep and the Goats (Matt. 25:32, 33).

TEARING THE PAPER

Now let us tear the paper, and let the two parts stand for the two roads.

(Tear as in Fig. 6, and put the large piece in one hand, and the small pieces in the other. Note that one small piece is torn off with the large. This piece should be shifted to the other hand.)

I want two boys to come up to hold the cardboard for me. (Unfold the Cross.)

We will paste this on the small card, the narrow one. It represents the narrow road, the road of the Christian which leads to heaven, for "the Way of the Cross leads home."

Let us look at the other road—the broad road that Jesus said leads us to destruction. Watch and see where this road leads to. (Quickly paste all the pieces on Fig. 9.) The broad road leads to hell.

EACH MUST CHOOSE THE ROAD HE WILL TAKE

Each of us must choose the road he will take. It must be one of these two, and as we choose, let us not forget the end of the road. If, when Jesus gathers the harvest, we are on the narrow road, beneath the Cross of Jesus, we will go to heaven, for we will then be as the wheat. (Write WHEAT on card.) If we are tares (write TARES), we will be on the broad road, with the lost.

Likewise, if we are good or bad fish, sheep or goats, we will go to the end of whatever road we have travelled.

Elijah said, "Why halt ye between two opinions? If God be God, follow Him" (I Kings 18:21).

John the Beloved Apostle made the right choice, and he went to heaven. Judas made the wrong choice, and he went to hell, so

"CHOOSE YOU THIS DAY WHOM YE WILL SERVE" (Josh. 24:15).

ADDITIONAL ILLUSTRATIONS

When Jesus told the story of the rich man and Lazarus, He said there was a great gulf fixed between the two men. That gulf cannot be bridged. None can pass from one to the other.

We have been able to cross the oceans with vessels and aeroplanes, and we have built great bridges across deep rivers, and roads have been built over the mountains so that we can travel in comfort over dangerous mountain passes. No task seems too difficult for our modern engineers, but the gulf that God has fixed between heaven and hell cannot be bridged by the best engineers, nor charted by the best navigators, nor crossed by the best pilots. Our choice today will put us on the right or wrong side of the chasm.

SOME ONE IS AT THE OTHER END

In a small southern town, each morning when the mail arrived, a group of mountain men gathered in the post-office to listen for their names to be called. Each morning disappointment came. A minister who was a stranger noticed that no mail ever came to them. He asked the postmaster if they had ever received a letter. The postmaster said, "No, you see, they don't understand that some one has to be at the other end to send the letter."

Well, a kind farmer heard about it; so one day he found out their names and sent each of them a letter. The next morning as their names were called out by the postmaster, and they answered to the call, they did what you are doing today. They all heard the call. Then they opened their letters and each received an invitation to come to spend the day at the home of the farmer. Some went and some did not, but all got an invitation.

Some one at the other end is inviting you today, to come to His house. You can read the letter and then throw it aside, or you can accept the invitation.

FiG.-1. ALIVE!

FiG-2. SOLDIERS

FiG.-3. STONE.

FiG.-4. SEAL.

FiG.-5. TOMB

FiG.-6. GRAVE CLOTHES

FiG.-7.

FiG.8. GRAVE CLOTHES

FiG.-9. GRAVE CLOTHES

TOMB

FiG.-10.

FiG.-11. ALIVE!

T.H.

IV

BREAKING THE BANDS OF DEATH *

(An Easter Lesson)

MATERIAL NEEDED—

Six envelopes of various sizes.
A half-dollar.
Crayon or paint.

CONSTRUCTION OF OBJECT—

1. Print the word ALIVE on the longest envelope. Fig. 1.
2. Print the word SOLDIERS on the next size. Fig. 2.

At the lower left hand corner, cut a slit in the envelope, large enough for the half-dollar to go through easily.

3. On the other envelopes, graded in size, print the words STONE, SEAL, TOMB, GRAVE CLOTHES. Cut slits in each of these in lower left hand corners. Figures 2 to 8.

If you cannot find enough different envelopes in size, to form the nest, make some with paper and glue.

WARNING

Do not cut a slit in the corner of the ALIVE envelope.

THE LESSON

Boys and girls, Easter is a glad, happy day, but the several days before Easter were days of sorrow, for Jesus was dead.

THE CAVE-TOMB

Jesus didn't die in a hospital in a soft bed, surrounded by friends, and cared for by tender hands. He died on a wooden cross, among His enemies.

After He was dead, Nicodemus and Joseph of Arimathæa came and asked for His body.

---

* Published in abbreviated form in *Church Management*.

Rich people always had their tombs all ready, long before they died. Jesus had no tomb, for He was poor.

But Joseph of Arimathæa had his tomb. It was cut into the rocks on a hillside, like a cave, instead of being under ground.

GRAVE-CLOTHES

This half-dollar will represent the body of Jesus. (Hold up half-dollar.) After Joseph and Nicodemus took the body of Jesus, they tenderly wrapped it in grave-clothes. (Put half-dollar in GRAVE-CLOTHES envelope, and be careful not to let it get near the slit corner, lest it roll out.)

THE TOMB

Jesus was crucified on a Friday; we call it "Good Friday." The Jewish Sabbath began at sundown on Friday night, and continued until Saturday night.

Since it was not lawful to work on the Sabbath, a very hasty burial was made, in the tomb of Joseph. (Put GRAVE-CLOTHES envelope inside the TOMB envelope.)

THE SEAL

After burial, it was customary to seal the tomb (Matt. 27:66). Two kinds of seals were used.

The Roman government had a seal. It was stamped on important papers and property. Since Jesus died as a prisoner of the Roman government, in all probability the mark of the Roman seal was placed on the tomb, to show that His death was ordered by the government.

The other way of sealing a tomb was to stretch a cord across the door, and to fasten both ends of the cord by sealing clay or wax and stamp it with the governor's seal. (Place TOMB envelope in SEAL envelope.)

THE ROUND STONE

Then they took a great round stone and rolled it in front of the door. The Bible tells us this tomb was a new one. Perhaps it was not completely finished, so the stone was used as a temporary door, to keep people out. (Place SEAL envelope in STONE envelope.)

THE SOLDIERS

Then Pilate ordered soldiers to guard the tomb for three days, so nobody could steal the body, for Jesus had said He would arise on the third day.

The soldiers walked up and down in front of the large stone that formed the door of this sealed tomb. (Put the entire nest of envelopes in the ALIVE envelope, keeping the printed side of the nest of envelopes toward the children, and the printed side of the ALIVE envelope towards you. Place the nest of envelopes near one end of the ALIVE envelope, to allow the coin to come out through the slits, without interference. (Fig. 10.)

NIGHT AND DARKNESS

(As you put the ALIVE envelope over the others, say that night had now come, and the soldiers and the stone and the seal and the tomb and the grave-clothes and the body of Jesus was covered with darkness.)

THE EARLY SABBATH MORNING

The Jewish Sabbath quickly passed from Friday night to Sunday morning. Very early on Sunday morning, kind women came to tenderly prepare the body of Jesus for final burial.

These women did not know, perhaps, about the soldiers and the stone and the seal. They only knew that the body of Jesus was in the tomb of Joseph of Arimathæa.

When they came close to the tomb, in the gray dawn, they saw, in the distance, a moving angel, glistening white. He was sitting on the great, round stone, but the stone was not in front of the door at all! It had been rolled away.

Quickly and fearfully, they all approached, and the angel said to them, "Don't be afraid. I know you are looking for Jesus who was crucified. He is not here, for He has risen from the dead, as He said He would. Run back and tell His friends, especially Peter. He is in Galilee, and there you will see Him again."

(As you give this last part, squeeze the edges of the nest of envelopes in your hand, allowing the half-dollar to roll through the slits, and into the ALIVE envelope. A gentle shaking and tilting will help to get the coin into place in the ALIVE envelope. Fig. 10.)

WHERE THEY FOUND JESUS

The women ran back and told all the friends what they had seen and heard. Peter and John came running to the tomb. When they arrived, they found the soldiers lying as dead, on the ground. (Take SOLDIERS envelope out.)

They saw the stone rolled away. (Take STONE envelope out.)

They found the seal broken. (Take SEAL envelope out.)

They went into the tomb, but found it empty. (Take TOMB envelope out.)

They came right to the grave-clothes, which were rolled up in a corner, and they, too, were empty. (Open the envelope to show it is empty.)

Jesus had risen from the dead. (Turn ALIVE envelope around, and take out the escaped coin, so the children can see it.)

This is the true Easter story of Jesus, who died on the Cross, and then broke the bands of death.

If Jesus could break all these bands, through soldiers and stone, and seal, and tomb and grave-clothes, and could be made alive again, I believe He can break the bands of every sin and temptation and habit that any boy or girl has, and that they, too, can be "made alive in Christ Jesus unto life everlasting."

ADDITIONAL ILLUSTRATIONS

"For as in Adam all die, even so in Christ shall all be made alive." I Cor. 15:22.

If a father is an American, and a mother is an American, and the children are born in America, the children will be Americans.

Likewise, if the father is a sinner and the mother is, too, the children will be. Therefore the Bible says, "because Adam died, so shall we," for we are his children.

But Jesus came to adopt us as His children; to take us away from Adam; to give us a new name, a new hope, a new home.

When we become willing to be the children of God, the last part of this verse is fulfilled. "For as in Adam all die, even so in Christ shall all be made alive."

If additional thoughts are desired, to amplify the thought of our relationship to Christ's resurrection, you can arrange a card with the words printed as follows:

```
HAPPIN E SS
      S A VIOUR
RESPON S IBILITY
 AFFLIC T ION
      D E ATH
  FUNE R AL
```

Be prepared to cut out of the chart the word EASTER. Easter is the final experience of the children of God as well as of those who are not the children of God. Some shall be raised unto life everlasting and some unto damnation.

THE CHART EXPLAINED

We are born and the early years are spent in the HAPPINESS of childhood, without care.

As we grow up we find Christ as our SAVIOUR.

Then we are ready for life's fuller RESPONSIBILITY.

The years pass and AFFLICTION overtakes us.

Then comes DEATH, followed by the FUNERAL.

Then what? (Cut out Easter.)

Easter comes!! Why?

"For as in Adam all die, even so in Christ shall all be made alive."

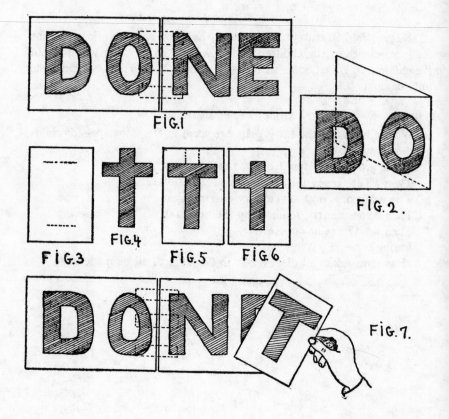

FIG.1

FIG.2.

FIG.3

FIG.4

FIG.5

FIG.6

FIG.7.

V

THE UNHAPPY HEATHEN

(A Missionary Lesson)

MATERIAL NEEDED—

Cardboard.
Gummed paper, or paper and glue.
Crayon or paint.
A paper clip.

CONSTRUCTION OF OBJECT—

1. Cut a piece of cardboard, 3½ x 7 inches. Print the word DONE upon it. Fig. 1.

2. Cut Fig. 1 apart, between O and N, and hinge these pieces together so the NE will fold back of DO. Fig. 2.

3. Cut another piece of cardboard 3½ x 1½ inches. Cut two slots in it. Fig. 3. The distance between these slots should be the same as the height of the letters in Fig. 1.

4. Cut out a cross, as in Fig. 4, and colour it the same colour of letters. Put the cross in slots of Fig. 3, making the letter T. When pulled down, it will show as a cross. Fig. 6.

5. Fasten Fig. 5 over the letter E with paper clip. Fig. 7. Now fold to position of Fig. 2, and proceed with lesson.

THE LESSON

DO

We think of the heathen across the sea, but there are also hundreds of thousands of heathen in our own land. They are the unhappy people who worship false gods.

There are many millions of heathen in India, China, Japan, Africa, Europe, the islands of the seas, etc.

Most of them believe in some kind of a life after death, but are mistaken as to how to get this eternal life. They believe they must *do* certain things to be saved. (Hold up DO.) In India, they often do the most terrible things in order (as they imagine) to obtain eternal peace.

They often crawl for miles upon their stomachs, for days and days, to get to some shrine, believing that, if they reach there, they will be saved by this sacrifice they have made. Many of them faint on the wayside under the sun, and the birds come and pluck out their eyes even before they die. If, and when, they reach the shrine, they sit on the steps and starve themselves to death, saying, "If we do this, we will be saved."

Others sit on a board with long spikes in it. How unhappy the heathen must be, to think they must do these painful things.

Over in those lands, when a baby is born, it is put in a smoky house, with charcoal burning, and the smoke often causes the little baby to go blind. This is a part of their religion. They do this to drive the evil spirits away, and to be saved.

In China, they take the girl babies and tie bandages tightly around their tiny feet, to keep the feet small, for large feet are a disgrace there. Many girls go through life crippled from this religious custom, for their feet are like babies' feet even when they grow old. They do all of this, as they say, to please their god.

OUR CIVILIZED HEATHEN

We have American heathen, too. They, too, want to do things to be saved. They say, "We will give much money, and we will win favour with God." Now the Bible teaches us that this is not the right way to be saved. We can't buy our way into favour with God, for we are already "bought with a price." "Ye are bought with a price, not with corruptible things such as silver and gold, but with the precious blood of Jesus."

Others want to earn their salvation by working for it. They want to do something to be saved. Again the Bible says, "For by grace are ye saved through faith, and that not of yourselves; it is the gift of God, not of works, lest any man should boast. Not by works of righteousness which we do, but by the washing of regeneration, and the renewing of the Holy Ghost."

THE MEN AT THE TEMPLE

Two men went to the temple to pray, Jesus said. It turned out that one of them went to brag. The bragger said, "Lord, I *do* many things.

I give one-tenth of all I earn, and twice each week I go without my dinner, and every day I offer so many prayers, etc."

The other man simply said, "Lord, I have nothing to offer. I have no money to give, I have never been a good man, I can't *do* anything for my salvation, but Lord, be merciful to me, a sinner."

Jesus said the first man who prayed and boasted that he could and did *do* so much was a heathen. He said the second man that cried for mercy and could *do* nothing, went away saved.

We must all come to Jesus like the man who sang,

"Nothing in my hand I bring,
Simply to Thy cross I cling."

DON'T—DON'T—DON'T!

There is also another group of heathen in America. They have a long, sour face, and some of them might be living right here in our own town. (Hold up DON'T.)

This is their byword—don't. Did you ever hear people say, "Don't?" Every time they say "Don't" I want to *do* it—don't you?

Well, they are good people, but they haven't found the real way of happiness and salvation. They declare we are saved by the things we don't do. Now we hope we can say to all of you, *"Don't* swear. *Don't* lie. *Don't* steal. *Don't* break the Sabbath. All of these "don'ts" are written in God's holy law, but we could obey all of these "don'ts" and yet not be happy. The rich young ruler lived up to all of these "don'ts." Then when Jesus said, "I am glad you don't do these sins, but I want you to take up your cross and follow Me, and you shall have life eternal," the young man turned away, sad at heart. He had a "don't" religion, but it did not save him.

THE RIGHT KIND OF RELIGION

DONE

(Take the T off the E and show DONE, holding the T in the other hand, forming it into a cross.)

If we want to be happy Christians, we must come to Jesus. We can't save ourselves by the things we *do,* and we can't save ourselves by the things we *don't.* The only way we can be saved is by accepting the thing that Jesus has done for us. Jesus died on the Cross. (Pull down Cross.) While dying He said, "It is finished, or it is done."

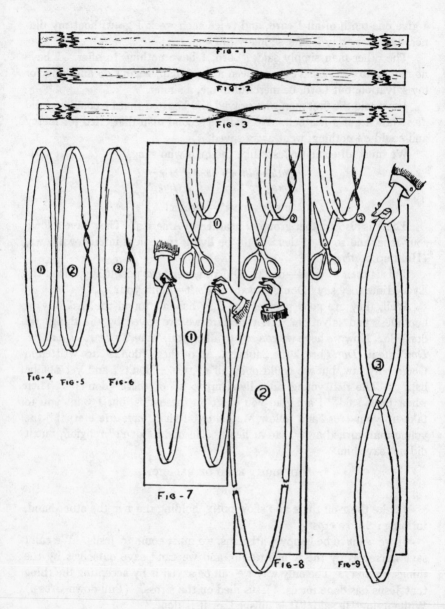

Fig-1

Fig-2

Fig-3

Fig-4   Fig-5   Fig-6

Fig-7

Fig-8   Fig-9

VI

"I'LL BET YOU A DIME"

(A strong lesson against gambling)

MATERIAL NEEDED—

    Crêpe paper, or a newspaper.

    Scissors.

    Glue.

    Several dimes.

CONSTRUCTION OF OBJECT—

    1. Cut three strips of paper three-fourths of an inch wide and about four feet long. Length can be attained by pasting several pieces together.

    2. Make a band like Fig. 4, glueing ends.

    3. Make a second band, Fig. 5, twisting the strip as in Fig. 2. (Two half-turns.)

    4. Make a third band, Fig. 6, giving it a half twist, as in Fig. 3.

    5. Mark the bands to identify them.

EFFECT

By cutting these bands, lengthways down the centre, three curious effects will result. The first band will make two separate bands. The second will make one large band. The third will form two bands, linked together.

You will need two younger boys to help you.

THE LESSON

Will you two boys help me today? I have a surprise lesson, with the promise of some easy money.

THE DIMES

Here I have two dimes. You can get one of these dimes for nothing. That's easy money, is it not? In order to get one of these dimes, you will have to have a dime of your own to begin with. Do either of you happen to have a dime all your own? Neither of you? Well, that's too bad.

THE BORROWED DIME

Well, I will loan you one of these dimes, and then you can pay me back. Here, son, you borrow the dime, and remember who you got it from. Now if you are lucky, you can win the other dime. Of course, you also take the chance of losing the dime you borrowed from me, for that is the way with all games of chance. It all depends on your luck.

THE FIRST BAND

Now I will show you how easily you can win my dime. Anybody could do it. Here is a paper band. It is made from last night's newspaper. There wasn't much in it, so it didn't hurt to cut it up. And here is a pair of scissors, which is like your dime—borrowed.

CUT THE BAND

Watch carefully, for I want you to do this when I get through.

I will cut the band right down the middle, making two bands. (Cut band as in Fig. 7). There, I have two bands now, and how easy that was.

I want you to take a band and cut it just like I did. Do you think you can do it? If you can, here is the band and scissors.

THE OVER-CONFIDENT BOY

You say you can do it? I would like to bet my dime against your dime that you can't do it. If you can do it, I will give you my dime, and if you don't do it, then you will give me your dime. That's fair, is it not, boys and girls? Sure.

All right, will you bet? You will.

THE STAKEHOLDER

Now (turning to the other boy) we have made a bet, and we will need your help. In every bet, somebody wins and somebody loses. The money is put up, and the stakeholder holds the money of both parties, and then later turns the money over to the winner. Would you act as stakeholder, and hold the money? If he cuts the band into two bands, you will give him the two dimes, but if he doesn't cut the band into two bands, you will give me the two dimes. All right, here is my dime, and you get his borrowed dime.

Now, Mr. Stakeholder, I am ready. And here, Mr. Betting-Man, is the band and the scissors. I will hold both up for all to see, before we begin. (Try to conceal the twist in your hand.)

THE BETTING-BOY CUTS THE BAND

Go ahead, and cut two bands out of one, like I did. Keep your mind on the band, and cut it straight down the centre. Here's hoping you lose, and I win.

I am very sorry I could not make the same offer to all of you, for this is going to be easy money—for somebody.

THE TERRIBLE MISTAKE

See, he is cutting the two bands, all right. I see my dime going. There, now he has finished, and there are the two bands. (Hold them up so all can see.) What? What have you done here? You don't have two bands. What is this, just one band, and twice as big as the first one? Why, my dear boy, you have made a terrible mistake. How did you do that?

HIS SURPRISE AND LOSS

You bet me a dime you could cut the band into two bands, like I did, and here you have gone and cut it into one band. You lose the bet, and the stakeholder should give me the two dimes.

ANOTHER CHANCE

I am very sorry for you. I will do what no other gambler ever did. I will give you another chance. This time be more careful, and cut the band exactly in the middle, and cut me two separate bands, just like I did.

Now, I am your friend, and I want to see you get along in the world, so I will make another bargain with you. I will loan you another dime. I will bet you another dime against your dime that you can't cut me another band like the one you just cut, and you can't cut me two bands, like the ones I cut. Will you bet? You will.

All right, Mr. Stakeholder, here is my dime, and here is the dime this boy borrows from me, and which he will pay back to me when he wins the stakes, if he does.

All right, cut the band. (Give him the band of Fig. 6).

A CHAT WITH THE CHILDREN WHILE HE CUTS

You know, boys and girls, this betting business was never very sure. You can never tell if you will win or lose. I won the first time, but I may lose this time.

I imagine this is the first bet this boy ever made in all his life, and I am hoping it will be the last.

BETTING IS GAMBLING

Betting is the worst form of gambling, and gambling always has some trick of deceit, whereby the regular gambler makes the other fellow lose.

Now, son, you have it just about finished, I see. There it is. Yes, sir, and there are the two bands, all cut, just like the ones I cut, and there goes my dime.

What—you have two bands, but they are linked together, and not separate like mine were? Horror of horrors, and you were so sure you could do it; so sure that you were willing to bet money on it, and borrowed money at that.

COLLECT THE STAKES

Mr. Stakeholder, he loses the money and I win. Give me the stakes.

THE BORROWED MONEY

Not only have you lost your bets, but you have lost the two dimes I loaned you. You owe me two dimes. Now don't feel badly about that, because I am going to help you out of that. You have been a big help to me today on the platform, so I am going to pay you. I will pay you two dimes, and then you can pay me back what you owe me, and we will be square. Here is your pay, and now I will take mine. Thank you for paying back what you borrowed.

For your kindness in helping me teach this lesson, I want you and the stakeholder to have this little gift. (Offer any little gift, for there has been much embarrassment, and perhaps some resentment on the part of the boy. You must remove this before you dismiss him, and make him feel he was one of the teachers in this lesson, rather than the victim of a trick.)

HIS FIRST AND LAST BET

By the way, I suppose this is the first bet you ever made? Yes? Well, I hope it will be the last,

BECAUSE BETTING IS GAMBLING, AND GAMBLING BRINGS LOSS AND SORROW.

ADDITIONAL ILLUSTRATIONS

We can gamble with things besides money, but no matter what the gamble is, the gambler always loses.

The people in the days of Noah gambled with the Flood, and lost their lives in the swirling waters 120 years later.

Judas gambled with the priests for thirty pieces of silver. The end of that gamble was that he threw the thirty pieces of silver on the floor of the temple and himself over a precipice.

Adam and Eve gambled with the judgment for a bite of fruit, and lost the Garden of Eden in a single game.

Holy things can be gambled with, but "Whatsoever a man soweth, that shall he also reap."

Gambling is the lowest form of professional laziness. It may look like a short cut to riches, but it is really a short cut to the prison or poor house.

Same may be applied to gambling with life for the soul after death

Josh. 24:15

II Timothy 2:11-13

Gal. 6:7-8

Matthew 7:13-14

44

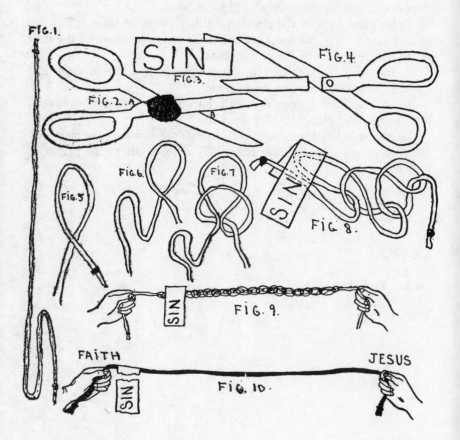

FIG.1.

SIN
FIG.3.

FIG.4.

FIG.2. A   B

O

Fig.5   Fig.6   Fig.7

SIN

FIG.8.

SIN   FIG.9.

FAITH   JESUS

SIN   FIG.10.

VII

CUT IT OUT

MATERIAL NEEDED—

One piece of heavy wrapping cord, four feet long.
Two pairs of ten-cent-store scissors.
One piece of gummed paper.
Crayon or paint.

CONSTRUCTION OF OBJECT—

1. Break off one point of scissors, just below the shaft. Filing would help, lest you break it at the shaft. Fig. 4.

2. Solder other pair, so they will not move. Fig. 2. Or get a ring from a loose-leaf notebook, and put it between the handles and cutting edges at points A and B in Fig. 2.

3. Print SIN on a gummed label, size 2 x 5 inches. Fig. 3.

4. Learn to tangle cord in a chain knot. (This is important.) Make an incomplete loop as in Fig. 5. Put another partial loop through first loop, as in Figs. 6 and 7. Put more partial loops through last loop each time. Fig. 7.

5. When you have made many loops, seal the single string with the last loop (Fig. 8), with the label SIN to hold it in place. Never put the end of the cord through any loop, or it will not unravel. When finished, it will look like Fig. 9.

6. If your tangle is correct, the cord will unravel when the ends are pulled on. Fig. 10.

SUGGESTION

Rehearse. If you prefer, you can make the tangle before coming to the teaching period, but it is preferable to do it before the children.

THE LESSON

Boys and girls sometimes like to use slang. I suppose some of you have pet slang phrases you like to use. Perhaps you have said, "Go, chase yourself," or "Take a jump into the lake," or "Oh, yeah?" or "So's your old man."

Perhaps somebody here has said sharply, when angry, "Cut it out," which in plain English means, "Stop it."

Well, "CUT IT OUT" is the title of our lesson today. You see I have brought two pairs of scissors to help us to "cut it out."

TWO BOYS NEEDED

I will need two boys to help me with the lesson. (Use younger boys, as older children often resent apparent ridicule, and this lesson may incur those helping you some slight embarrassment.)

THE CORD

I have a long cord here, and this represents your life. Of course I hope your life will be longer than this string.

THE HANDS REPRESENT TEMPTATIONS

My hands will represent TEMPTATIONS. If we get too friendly with temptation, we will fall into sin. My hands can tangle this cord all up with loops and knots. That is exactly what Satan does with our lives. He tangles them all up with sin.

THE TANGLED LIFE

I will show you what I mean. Here is a cord without a knot or tangle in it. Oh, excuse me, it *does* have a knot or two on the ends. A knot on the end of a rope has saved many a man's life. When you come to the end of the rope (to use another slang expression), tie a knot on the end and hang on.

I am going to tangle this cord all up. When I have it finished, it will look just like your life looks to God, when it is all tangled up with sin.

HABITS

All of us have some habits, and some of them are *bad* habits. Some boys and girls say, "I don't care if I do have bad habits, because I can *cut them out* any time I want to." Don't be fooled into believing that, boys and girls, because you *can't* always cut them out.

CONTINUE WITH LOOPS AND SHOW OCCASIONALLY

This loop represents the first lie. This one the first act of disobedience to mother. This one, breaking the Sabbath. This one, saying bad words. This one, stealing. Say, this boy is getting his life into a terrible tangle.

He says he doesn't care, because he can cut it out any time he wants to.

CIGARETTES AND LIQUOR

Many a boy, when he smoked his first cigarette, never intended to become a slave to tobacco. He said, "I can cut it out any time I want to." He developed the appetite for tobacco, and soon it became his master.

Others take the first glass of liquor. They promise themselves never to become drunkards; but soon after the first glass, they are helpless victims—slaves to the tangle of sin.

THE SINNER'S SURPRISE PARTY

All of these things I have mentioned are more than habits. They are *sins*. (Hold up SIN label.)

Sin will tie and bind us up, until we are helpless. (Seal the label over end loop.)

How surprised people are when they find themselves slaves to some sin! They say, "It is high time for me to begin to cut out some of my bad habits." Then they have a big surprise, for they find the tangle is not so *easily* cut out.

Now, my boy, I want you to help me. Do you think you can cut out the tangle? You think you can. I always admire a boy who says he can do things. Well, here is the scissors, and you cut out the tangle right here where it begins. (Hand him scissors of Fig. 2.)

There, now cut it. What seems to be the matter? You say it *won't* cut? The scissors are fastened?

Well, I *am* surprised; but I am no more surprised than many will be when they try to cut out their bad habits and sins.

THE OTHER SCISSORS AND THE OTHER BOY

Perhaps the other boy can help me out. If I give you a different pair of scissors, do you think you can cut the tangle out? Sure.

Come right here, and I will give you this pair. Now you cut out the bad habits and sin of this tangled life. (Give him scissors of Fig. 4.)

What? You can't do it, either? The scissors are broken?

Well, well, well, cutting it out is not so easy, after all, is it?

IT CAN'T BE CUT OUT

We will have to give it up, I guess, for I have no more scissors. We have tried and failed. We just *can't* cut it out.

THERE IS A BETTER WAY

I am afraid many of you who have bad habits and sins will meet with the same disappointment if you depend on the cut-it-out way. (Hold up one hand, showing five fingers.) How many fingers have I here? Five. I want to give you a five-letter word—one letter for each finger.

F-A-I-T-H

The letters spell FAITH. Now, listen. If we have our lives all tangled up with sin, and we haven't the power to cut sin out ourselves, then we ought to let somebody else do it for us. In order to do this, we must have *faith in somebody else.*

If you were sick and needed an operation, you wouldn't let me operate on you, because I am not a doctor, and you would have no faith in me, for I know nothing about operations. You would find a doctor in whom you had faith. You must have the same kind of faith in somebody else, who is able to cut out your sin. You must believe and trust Him, just like you do your doctor.

I would like to introduce you to One who can do this. His name has five letters in it, one letter for each finger of my other hand. It is

J-E-S-U-S

If I have faith in Jesus, He can cut out the sin from my life. "If we confess our sins, He is faithful and just to forgive our sins, and to cleanse us from all unrighteousness" (1 John 1:9).

Here, then, is my life. I will give it to Jesus. (Put one end of the cord in one hand.) Now I have faith to believe that Jesus is able to take away my sin. (Put other end of tangled cord in other hand.)

WATCH CAREFULLY

I am about to let Jesus, and my faith in Him, break the sin that holds me a slave. (Give a sharp pull, and the cord will untangle.)

Do you see, boys and girls? There is a better way to get rid of sin than to cut it out. Let Jesus take your life into His hand, and have faith to believe that He can help. He will take out the tangle.

A WORD TO THE TWO BOYS

Thank you, boys, for helping me to teach the lesson, today. I am afraid I fooled you with the scissors, but we will still be friends, won't we? You go home and tell your father and mother that you were the teachers today, who helped us learn the truth, that it is better to let God *blot out* sin than to try to cut it out ourselves.

50

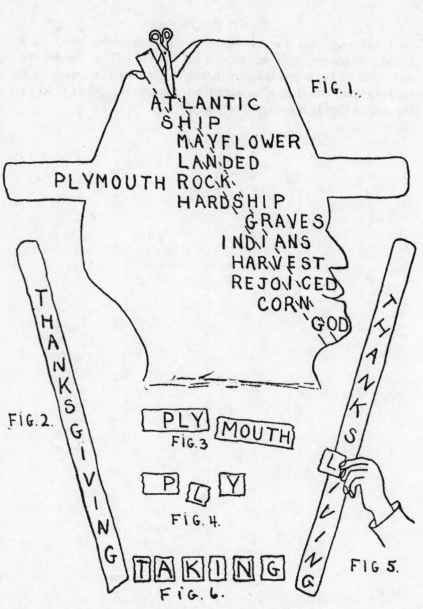

ATLANTIC
SHIP
MAYFLOWER
LANDED
PLYMOUTH ROCK
HARDSHIP
GRAVES
INDIANS
HARVEST
REJOICED
CORN
GOD

FIG. 1.

FIG. 2.

THANKSGIVING

PLY MOUTH
FIG. 3.

P L Y
FIG. 4.

THANKS LIVING

FIG 5.

TAKING
FIG. 6.

VIII

THE FIRST THANKSGIVING *

MATERIAL NEEDED—

A large piece of white wrapping-paper.

Crayon or paint.

Scissors.

CONSTRUCTION OF OBJECT—

1. Upon the wrapping-paper, print the words as shown in Fig. 1.

2. As a cutting guide, mark with a pencil, very faintly, around the word THANKSGIVING.

3. Around the words, draw a profile of a Pilgrim's face. If this seems hard, make only a Pilgrim's hat.

THE LESSON

To most of us, Thanksgiving means a day of vacation from school, attendance at football games, and turkey dinners. To our Pilgrim Fathers it meant much more. Over three hundred years ago, a group of people became dissatisfied in their own country, and this is what brought about the FIRST THANKSGIVING.

A group of about one hundred brave men and women, who loved God, set out from England to America. A great body of water lies between these two lands. It is the ATLANTIC Ocean. (Point to these words on the profile as you proceed.)

THE SHIP

To cross the ocean, a SHIP had to be used. In those days there were no large ships like we have today. The only ship they could get for this dangerous voyage was the MAYFLOWER.

LANDED AT PLYMOUTH ROCK

After many, many weeks of trial and battle against the storms at sea,

* Published in *Church Management* in abbreviated form.

these brave Pilgrims landed in the new country, where they could worship God according to the way they believed. The place they LANDED on was a great rock. It is called PLYMOUTH ROCK, and it was named after the place from which they had set out—Plymouth, England.

HARDSHIPS AND GRAVES

They landed in winter. It was December, in 1620, and since they had no homes and shelter, they had to endure many HARDSHIPS. During the first six months in this new land, they had to dig about fifty GRAVES, in which to put those who had died, and this was about half the number of all the people.

INDIANS

They suffered greatly from hunger and cold and sickness. Among the enemies they had to deal with were the redskins—the INDIANS. There was much blood shed, and many were killed.

HARVEST

Then came the celebration of the first Thanksgiving. They had sown their seed, and had asked God to keep them alive, until they could raise grain for bread. They lived on wild turkeys and meat they had hunted. During the first summer, following the hard winter months, the grain grew, and then in the autumn, they had a great HARVEST.

THEY REJOICED

All the people REJOICED. They had been facing starvation and death, and now all were happy, for they had grain for bread.

THE CORN

Their main food was CORN. When they had gathered in all of their corn, and the harvest was over, and they were well supplied for the winter, they remembered they had asked God for help.

GOD

Hence, they set one day, in which all were to gather, to worship GOD and celebrate with thanksgiving. On that day, everything was put aside, all work was left, and they came together for the first Thanksgiving.

CUT OUT THANKSGIVING

The Pilgrims had thanksgiving even in their faces, they were so happy and grateful. Of course they had it in their hearts, too. All through their experiences, crossing the Atlantic in the small ship, the MAYFLOWER, and landing at Plymouth Rock, undergoing hardship, digging graves, fighting Indians, sowing seed and reaping the harvest of corn, they had THANKS-GIVING. (Cut out the word here. Fig. 2.)

NOT ONLY MOUTH-THANKSGIVING

(Take the word Plymouth, and cut out the word MOUTH. Fig. 3.) Some people thank God with the mouth only. Some say thanks at the table, and then grumble because the food does not suit them. It is fine for you boys and girls to say "Thanks" to God when you sit down to the table. Ask your mother to teach you a prayer of "Thanks." If she hesitates, tell her that even a pig grunts when it gets something to eat.

THANKSGIVING SHOULD BE THANKSLIVING

(Cut the L out of PLY, as in Fig. 4, and hold it over the G, as in Fig. 5, spelling THANKSLIVING.) Some people celebrate THANKSGIVING only once a year, on a Thursday in November. God wants more than this. If we give thanks we should also *live* thanks. We should show Him as well as tell Him. If we give thanks and then do not live thanks, God will say, "What you *do* speaks so loudly, I cannot hear what you *say*."

TAKING AND GIVING

(Cut up the word thanksgiving, saving the letters TAKING. Have six children come and hold the letters for you, in order.) Many people are always *taking* things from God, but are never *giving*. Once there were ten men who were lepers, who came to Jesus to be healed, and He healed them all. Of the ten, only *one* returned to thank Him. The other nine were the *taking* kind, not the *giving* kind, for they never even returned to give Him thanks.

Taking things *from* God and never giving things *to* God, is the height of ingratitude, and is not in keeping with the spirit of the FIRST THANKS-GIVING of the Pilgrim Fathers.

54

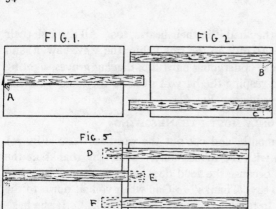

FIG.1. FIG.2. FIG.4.

A B C

FIG.5 D E F

FIG.3.

FIG 6. FAR COUNTRY FIG 7.

BAD COMPANIONS   DRUNKARDS   GAMBLERS

FIG 8.

FAMINE   PIG PEN   CORN HUSKS

FATHERS HOUSE   KISS

RING   ROBE

FIG.10.   FIG.9.   FIG 11

FEAST   SHOES

IX

FROM A POT OF GOLD TO A PEN OF PIGS

The Story of the Prodigal Son (LUKE 15)

MATERIAL NEEDED—

Cardboard.
Tissue-paper.
Glue.
Envelopes.
Crayon or paint.

CONSTRUCTION OF OBJECT—

1. Cut two pieces of cardboard, 3 x 5 inches. Figs. 1 and 2.
2. Cut three strips of tissue-paper, ½ x 6½ inches. Fig. 3.
3. Lay tissue-strips on cards, as in Figs. 1 and 2. Bend over the ends of strips at A, B, C, and glue down the ends on bottom side of cards.
4. Place cards together and slip loose ends of the tissue-strips in place, and glue to under sides of cards, as in Fig. 5.

NOTE

The ends only of the tissue-strips are pasted, and these on the under side at dotted lines D, E, F.

5. Cut a piece of tissue-paper, 2 x 7 inches, and fold it into three-eighths inch pleats. Fig. 4.
6. Paste this pleated fold to object with one end of fold on tissue-strip and other end on bare card. Fig. 6.
7. Mark one end of the card to differentiate it from the other end, so that, when manipulated, the fold will appear and disappear, while holding those respective ends.
8. Print FAR COUNTRY on a large envelope.
9. On six pieces of light weight cardboard, print the words, BAD COM-PANIONS, DRUNKARDS, GAMBLERS, FAMINE, PIG-PEN, CORN-HUSKS. Fig. 8. Place these in order in the FAR COUNTRY envelope.

10. Print FATHER'S HOUSE on another large envelope.

11. On five other cards, print KISS, RING, ROBE, FEAST, SHOES. Place these in order in the FATHER'S HOUSE envelope.

THE LESSON

I want to tell you the story of a boy who started with a pot of gold and ended in a pen of pigs. Jesus called him The Prodigal Son, and the story is found in the fifteenth chapter of Luke's Gospel.

WHAT THE BOY HAD

The Prodigal's father was very wealthy, so the boy had everything he wanted. (Hold up object with fold in sight.) I want this beautiful fold to represent the many things he had, such as money, a nice home, many friends, much happiness, a good reputation. Let us all say it together. He had MONEY, HOME, FRIENDS, HAPPINESS, REPUTATION.

THE FAR COUNTRY

He had been a good boy. He had worked for his father and obeyed his mother, and loved his older brother. Then he heard about the FAR COUNTRY. (Hold up that envelope.) He thought about it in the day time and dreamed about it at night. Finally he went to his father and asked him for his share of the money, which would some day be his, begging that he might go to the Far Country and have a good time while he was still young.

HE LEAVES HOME

The father loved his boy, and begged him not to go, warning him of the dangers of the Far Country. He told him that many evil things were hidden in the Far Country. However, the boy persuaded the father to give him the money and let him go. With everything packed, he bade his father and mother and brother "Good-bye." (Fold up object and place in the FAR COUNTRY envelope.)

WHAT HE FOUND IN THE FAR COUNTRY

1. BAD COMPANIONS

Soon he reached the borders of the Far Country. There he fell in with bad companions. Under evil influence of these wicked men, he fell in with

2. DRUNKARDS

Wishing to be a good fellow, he took his first drink of liquor. Soon he, too, was a drunkard. (Show these cards, as you develop each point.)

GAMBLERS

The bad companions and drunkards laid plans to get his money away from him. They introduced him to some gamblers. (Show card.) They suggested that they play for his money, telling him that if he was lucky, he could win their money from them, and then he would be twice as rich. So he gambled and lost. When his money was gone, his friends left him, and he soon found himself a poor, ragged, homeless boy.

THE GREAT FAMINE

Then a great famine arose, and many people were hungry, for there was not enough to eat in the Far Country. (Show FAMINE card.) He thought about his father and home, where there was plenty to eat.

THE PIG-PEN

He tramped through the country, begging for a bite to eat. Everywhere he went, he asked for a job. One farmer told him he could go out and take care of the pigs. This was the worst job he could have found, for he was a Jewish boy, and the Jews call pigs unclean, and to this very day will not eat pork. (Show PIG-PEN card.)

THE CORN-HUSKS

While taking care of the pigs, he ate with them, perhaps even eating the husks of corn. (Show CORN-HUSKS card.) One day while he was doing this he suddenly

CAME TO HIMSELF

After finding all of these in the Far Country—bad companions, drunkards, gamblers, famine, pig-pens, corn-husks, he came to himself and said, "What have I done? I had money, home, friends, happiness, and a good reputation." (Take object out of the envelope and open it so the fold does not appear. Fig. 10.) "Now all of these are gone, for I have lost them through my foolish disobedience to my dear father and mother, and through my sin and wickedness. How foolish I have been."

HE GOES BACK HOME

Then he decided to go back home, back to the father's house. (Show

FATHER'S HOUSE envelope. Fold up the object again, and this time place it in the FATHER'S HOUSE envelope.)

THE KISS

While he was still a far ways off, his father saw him, and came and met him and planted a kiss of love on his brow. (Take KISS card out of envelope.) This was a sign the father still loved him.

THE RING

Then the father took him into the house and put a ring on his finger. (Show RING card.) This was the sign that he was to be a part of the family again, and they were to be as one, just as the bride and groom become one at the wedding, when the man puts the ring on the bride's finger. The ring is a complete circle, and has no end. So the love of the father for the Prodigal was to have no end.

THE ROBE

The father called the servants in and ordered them to take off his swill-bespattered robe, and to give him a new robe. (Show ROBE card.) This was the sign that all the past was forgiven, for he was to be like a new son, with a new robe.

THE FEAST

The father also had the servants kill the fatted calf for a great feast. The neighbours came and there was a party with music. (Show FEAST card.) This was a sign that the Prodigal was to be restored to his friends and neighbours.

THE SHOES

The father ordered shoes to be put on his feet. (Show SHOES card.) This was a sign that he was to be a worker again, in the field, for shoes were worn only in the field, and never in the house.

LOST, BUT FOUND

The father was happy. He said, "My son was lost, but is found." (Take object out of FATHER'S HOUSE envelope, and open it so fold appears.) This fold stands for what he had before he went away to the Far Country of sin. He lost all he had while there, but when he came back to the father's house, he got it all back again.

Many of us may be in the far country away from the father's house.

We may have bad companions. We may be near the pig-pen and corn-husks. Jesus has said—and He is the head of the Father's house—"Whosoever cometh unto Me, I will in no wise cast out" (John 6:37).

If you will turn back from the Far Country, He will meet you and give you a kiss and a ring and robe and feast and shoes, and He will restore you to your friends, and He will keep you in His Father's house forever.

60

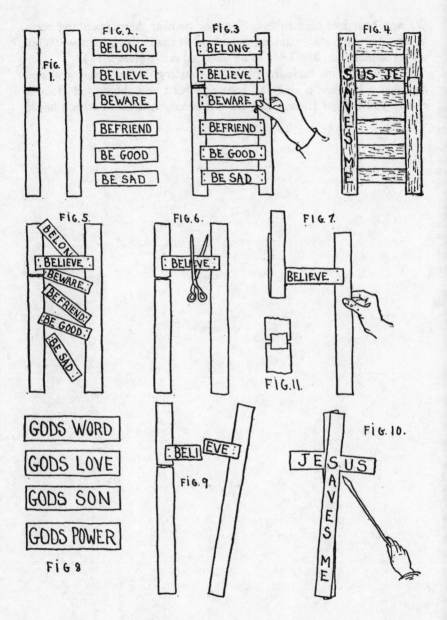

FIG. 1.

FIG. 2.
BELONG
BELIEVE
BEWARE
BEFRIEND
BE GOOD
BE SAD

FIG. 3.
: BELONG :
: BELIEVE :
: BEWARE :
: BEFRIEND :
: BE GOOD :
: BE SAD :

FIG. 4.
SAVES ME
SUS JE

FIG. 5.
BELONG
: BELIEVE :
: BEWARE :
: BEFRIEND :
: BE GOOD :
: BE SAD :

FIG. 6.
: BELIEVE :

FIG. 7.
BELIEVE :

FIG. 11.

GODS WORD
GODS LOVE
GODS SON
GODS POWER

FIG 8

FIG. 9.
: BELI EVE :

FIG. 10.
JESUS
SAVES ME

X

THE LADDER TO HEAVEN

MATERIAL NEEDED—

Cardboard.
Glue.
Paper.
Scissors.
Crayon or paint.

CONSTRUCTION OF OBJECT—

1. Cut two cardboard pieces, 2 x 20 inches. Fig. 1.
2. Cut six pieces and print words of Fig. 2 on them.
3. Make ladder with these parts. Fig. 3.
4. Cut left upright piece, just under BELIEVE. Fig. 3. Make a hinge on back of these pieces with glue and paper. Fig. 11.
5. On back of ladder, print words as in Fig. 4, so that when Fig. 10 is made, the words will line up to read JESUS SAVES ME.
6. Prepare four cards, with words printed as in Fig. 8.
7. Take scissors into pulpit with you.

THE LESSON

All through the ages, people have wanted to go to heaven. Many people have already gone there. Perhaps someone here has a mother, or father, or brother, or sister, or grandmother, or grandfather there. You will never see them again until you get there.

THE TOWER OF BABEL

I have a ladder with steps here. Many people are climbing up these steps, hoping they may reach heaven this way.

In the eleventh chapter of Genesis we are told that the people built a high tower, hoping that the top of it might reach to heaven. This was a false way to heaven, so God destroyed the tower and scattered the people and confused their language. They called this the Tower of Babel, but nobody ever reached heaven through that tower.

JACOB'S LADDER

The Book of Genesis (chap. 28) also tells us that one night Jacob went to sleep on the hillside. He used stones for pillows. In his dream he saw a ladder whose top reached to heaven, and he saw angels walking up and down on this ladder.

In the morning, Jacob awoke to find it was only a dream-ladder, so Jacob did not get to heaven on the ladder he saw.

A LONG LADDER WITH FALSE STEPS

I wonder if we can get to heaven by climbing this ladder? Jesus said something about people trying to climb up to heaven. (See John 10.) He said He was the Door of the sheepfold, and he that climbs up some other way, the same is a thief and a robber.

Some people say that to go to heaven, you must come up this first step and *be sad*. You must have a long, unhappy face, so long that you could eat oatmeal out of an ice cream freezer. Jesus said, "Be of good cheer, I have overcome the world." He wants us to be the happiest people on earth, because we are on our way to heaven.

GRANDPA AND THE LONG-FACED MULE

A little girl was converted. She ran home to tell her long-whiskered Grandpa. Her face beamed with happiness, but her Grandpa sadly said, "Oh, no, Granddaughter, you do not have Jesus in your heart, or you wouldn't laugh so much; you would be more solemn and sad, like Grandpa."

Sadly she went out to the barnyard, and there stood the old mule, lazy and long-faced. She talked to the old mule, and stroked its long face and said, "Maud, you must be a wonderful Christian, for you have such a long face."

No, children, this step—be sad—will not take us to heaven. We will cut it off the ladder, for it is a false step. (Cut off BE SAD.)

BE GOOD

Here is another step. Some say that if you want to go to heaven, just be *good*. The old Pharisees of the day of Jesus tried to get to heaven that way. They said to Jesus, "We are so good that we give one-tenth of our money to the poor, and sometimes eat only two meals a day to obey our religious laws."

Jesus was disgusted with them because their goodness was just on the outside. Their hearts were full of wickedness. Jesus called them sinners and hypocrites. He said they were like graves, very pretty on the outside, but full of dead men's bones inside. Isaiah 64:6 tells us that all our goodness is like filthy rags in God's sight. We will have to cut off that step, too, for the "be good" step is a false step. (Cut off BE GOOD.)

BEFRIEND

Others say that to get to heaven, we must *befriend* the strangers, the poor and the dumb animals. We should do all that, but that will not take us to heaven. Many people who befriend the stranger and the poor and the dumb animals hate God. They show that they hate Him by rejecting His Son. "Befriend" is a false step, so we will have to cut that out. (Cut out BEFRIEND.)

BEWARE

Some think all we need to do to go to heaven is to *beware* of a lot of things. To those péople, about half of life is poison. They want us to throw a lot out of our lives and hearts, and then never put anything in place, thus leaving an empty, unhappy heart.

In the eleventh chapter of Luke it is recorded that once a man lived in a house with an evil spirit and he tried to beware of all evil spirits, so he chased him out of his house. Then he swept it clean, so the house was beautiful.

The evil spirit could find no place to live, so he came back to the house and, finding it so clean, decided he would not only go back, but that he would bring seven other evil spirit friends with him. They all went to live in the man's house, so the last state of that man was worse than the first, and all because he wanted to beware. He cast him out, *but he left his house empty,* so the evil spirit came back with seven others.

The evil spirits were his bad habits. If we cast them out and put nothing in their place, they will come back. I want you to cast out of your house all the bad habits, but I also want you to let Jesus move in, so your house will not be empty. Martin Luther one day pointed to his heart and said, "Martin Luther doesn't live here any more. Martin Luther has moved out, and Jesus has moved in."

Just to *beware* of bad habits, and to *beware* of sin, and to *beware* of bad companions is not enough to take us to heaven. This is a false step, so we will cut it out. (Cut out BEWARE.)

BELONG

Here is a step, clear up on the top of the ladder—BELONG. Belong to *what?* Some say that if you *belong* to Church or Sunday School, or to the Young People's Society, you will go to heaven.

Everybody wants to belong to something. Will Rogers said that we are a nation of "Joiners"—that when two Americans meet on the street, one of them pulls a gavel out of his pocket and calls the other to order, for a meeting.

Belonging to the Church will not save us. We should belong to Church, not to *be* saved, but because we *are* saved. (Cut out this false step.)

BELIEVE

Now we have just one more step left—BELIEVE. This is the only true step in the ladder to heaven. Paul said to the Philippian gaoler, "Believe on the Lord Jesus Christ, and thou shalt be saved" (Acts 16:31).

One day Martin Luther was crawling up a flight of steps on his hands and knees. He had sinned, and this was his punishment. He believed that by doing this he would go to heaven. As he counted the steps he said, "There are fourteen more steps between me and heaven." A voice said to his heart, "There is only *one* step between you and heaven. Believe on the Lord Jesus Christ, and thou shalt be saved, for the just shall live by faith."

That day Luther took that one step and was saved.

WHAT MUST I BELIEVE?

Some of you are saying, "Is that all, just *believe?*" Yes. What must you believe? Well, you are to believe a number of things, so I will make a number here. (Make a number 4 as in Fig. 7. Do this by bending the hinged piece up.)

1. You must believe GOD'S WORD. It says, "All have sinned and come short of the glory of God."

2. You must believe GOD'S LOVE. Even though you have sinned, God loves you. "For God so *loved*, etc." (John 3:16).

3. You must believe in GOD'S SON. His name is Jesus and He came to save you from your sins. "God gave His only begotten Son, that whosoever believeth in Him should not perish, but have everlasting life."

4. You must believe GOD'S POWER. You have tried to climb the ladder to heaven by the following:

Be sad;

Beware;

Befriend;

Belong;

Be good.

None of these could save you. Only GOD has power to save you.

A LONG STEP CUT IN HALF

Here is your ladder to heaven, with but one step on it. BELIEVE. You say it is a long step up there; it is so high on the ladder. It *is* high, but that is because it is so near to heaven.

When the Prodigal Son came home, his father went out to meet him. Jesus will do that for you. He will come half-way, and thus cut the step in two. (Cut step with scissors, as in Fig. 9.)

Now that the step is cut in two, Jesus will meet you at the foot of the Cross, at the place where He showed you His great love. (Put the two pieces of Fig. 9 together, as in Fig. 10, and turn it around so lettering will show.)

If you will come to this ladder, and accept the only way to heaven, and *believe* in Jesus, you will be saying, "Jesus saves me."

> "*At the Cross, at the Cross, where I first saw the light,*
> *And the burden of my heart rolled away;*
> *It was there by faith, I received my sight,*
> *And now I am happy all the day.*"

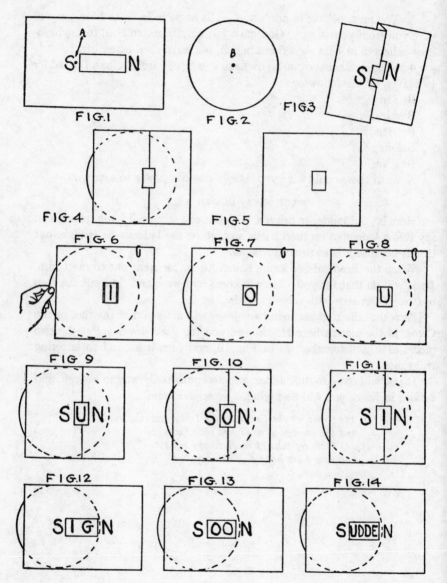

FIG.1   FIG.2   FIG3

FIG.4   FIG.5

FIG.6   FIG.7   FIG.8

FIG 9   FIG.10   FIG.11

FIG.12   FIG.13   FIG.14

XI

YOUR FIRST LOVE-LETTER

MATERIAL NEEDED—

Cardboard that will bend. (Postcard stock is good.)

A paper-clip.

A paper-fastener.

Black crayon or paint.

CONSTRUCTION OF OBJECT—

1. Cut the cardboard into a piece, 10 x 7½ inches.

2. Mark an oblong figure 1½ inches wide and 3¼ inches long. Fig. 1. This should be centred with a margin 3 inches from top edge, and 3 inches from bottom of card-edge. It should be 3¾ inches from the left edge and 2¾ inches from the right edge.

3. Cut this oblong figure out with a razor-blade.

4. ¼ inch from the left edge of the cut-out, make a small hole for the paper-fastener. See A in Fig. 1.

5. Print s and N as in Fig. 1.

6. Make a round disc, 7¼ inches in diameter, out of cardboard. See Fig. 2. Make small hole in the centre at B.

7. Fold Fig. 1 so the opening will be 1 inch wide, and 1½ inches high. See Figs. 3 and 4.

8. Put the disc back of Fig. 3, with paper-fastener through the holes A and B.

9. With the disc in place, print on it, through the opening, the letter I. Then turn the disc and print the letter O. Turn again and print U. Figs. 6, 7, 8.

10. Unfold Fig. 4 to full length, and print a G back of the I. Fig. 12. Turn the disc and print o back of o. Fig. 13. Then print DDE back of the u. Fig. 14. Fold this Fig. 14 back to position of Fig. 6.

11. Get another piece of cardboard, 7½ x 7½ inches. Place it over Fig. 6, and cut out spaces in Fig. 5, congruent to space in Fig. 6. Fasten in place with the paper-clip, and you are ready for the Lesson.

THE LESSON

Did you ever hear of a love-letter? I want to teach you who your first love-letter should be sent to.

Love-letters sometimes close with the words, "with my love." Love always finds a way to express itself. God loves us, but instead of writing us a love-letter, to tell us, He sent His dear Son to show us.

Jesus Himself said, "Greater love hath no man than this, that a man lay down his life for his friends."

Paul said, "God commendeth His love toward us, in that while we were yet sinners, Christ died for us."

If Christ loved us enough to be willing to die for our sins, I think we should love Him, and we should not be ashamed to tell Him so; so our first love-letter should be to Him.

> *"Everyone ought to love Jesus, Jesus,*
> *He died on the Cross to save us from sin,*
> *Everyone ought to love Jesus."*

THREE LITTLE LETTERS

There are three important words in this lesson, and each word has just one letter. Watch carefully so you can repeat them for me. Here they are. (Turn dial slowly to the letters—I O U.

Let us say them slowly. "I-O-U." Now faster. What is that you say? "I owe you?" That is exactly what I want you to write to Jesus. I OWE YOU. And when you add the words, "my love," it will be your first love-letter. I O U MY LOVE.

THREE REASONS FOR LOVING GOD

(Remove the shield, showing Fig. 9.) You can truly say to God, "I owe You my love, because You sent me the beautiful sun." Without it, life would be very dreary. Without flowers, light, heat, fruit, corn, etc.

The sun shines in all places some of the time. "It is always morning, some place in the world." When it is night in one place, it is morning some place else.

You can also truly say, "I owe my love to You, because You sent Your only begotten Son." (Show this by turning the dial.)

He came not only as a friend or teacher, or healer, but to die for me, as a Saviour.

You can say, "I owe You my love because You came to forgive my sin." (Turn dial to show the word SIN.)

JESUS STILL LOVES US AND WILL COME FOR US

After Jesus died, He was buried, but He arose again from the dead. Then He went back to heaven. A great cloud took Him up there, and while the disciples were looking upward in wonder, an angel came and said, "Why do you stand looking up into heaven like that? Jesus is gone, but He will come back again, sometime, for He still loves you." I hope you will be ready when He comes.

(Open up the fold to full length. Fig. 12.)

Many are asking for a sign to prove that He is coming back. They will not believe unless they have a sign. The Bible tells us we shall not have a sign. When Jesus comes back, He will come as a thief in the night—without any sign or warning.

(Turn dial to Fig. 13.)

Jesus may be coming back *soon*. We can't tell *how* soon, but it may be *real* soon. We should all be ready for Him, even if He should come today.

(Turn dial to Fig. 14.)

The Bible tells us His coming will be *sudden*. "Watch ye, therefore, for ye know neither the day nor the hour wherein the Son of man cometh." Will you be ready for Him?

> *"Oh, can you say you are ready, brother,*
> *Ready for the soul's bright home?*
> *Say, will He find you and me still watching,*
> *Waiting, when the Lord shall come?"*

70

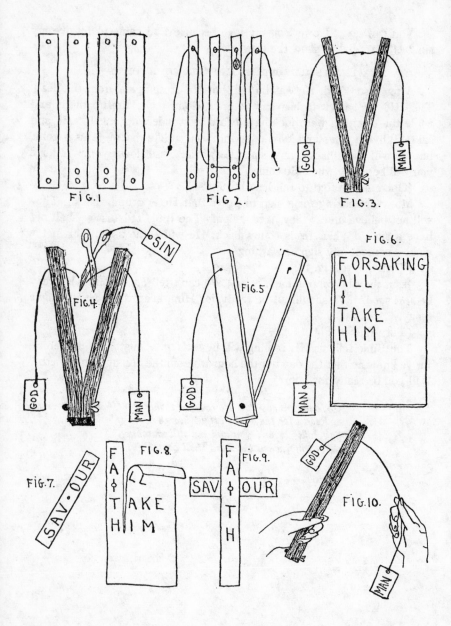

FIG.1

FIG.2

FIG.3

GOD   MAN

FIG.4

SIN

GOD   MAN

FIG.5

GOD   MAN

FIG.6.

FORSAKING
ALL
I
TAKE
HIM

FIG.7.

SAV·OUR

FIG.8.

FAITH

TAKE
HIM

FIG.9.

FAITH

SAV OUR

FIG.10.

GOD

MAN

XII

GOD IS LOST

MATERIAL NEEDED—

Heavy cardboard.

Sealing tape, or gummed paper.

String.

Scissors.

Paper-fasteners.

Crayon or paint.

CONSTRUCTION OF OBJECT—

1. Cut four pieces of cardboard, 1½ x 5 inches, and punch holes in them. Fig. 1.

2. Put a long string through the holes. Fig. 2.

3. Put a short string, 2 inches long, through top holes of the two middle pieces, and fasten ends of string down with gummed paper. Fig. 2.

4. Put paper-fastener through four bottom holes. Fig. 3.

5. Wrap sealing tape around the two left side strips, and then do same with the right side, making object look like two solid pieces. Fig. 5.

6. Put tags on the ends of the string, with words, GOD—MAN. Fig. 5.

7. Make a cardboard sign, as in Fig. 6, with words—FORSAKING ALL I TAKE HIM. Fig. 6.

8. Make a cardboard strip with the letters, SAV OUR. Fig. 7.

9. Put Fig. 7 back of Fig. 6 with a paper-fastener, through hole at I in Fig. 6, holding the two together.

10. Put a SIN tag on a pair of scissors. Fig. 4.

THE LESSON

I want to tell you a true story. It happened in Chicago in a large store on Van Buren Street, down in the heart of the loop, or downtown district.

A little girl went, with her father and mother, to this great store to see Santa Claus. There were thousands of people jammed and milling about that Santa Claus.

71

The little girl got her eyes upon the toys all over the store, and she got so interested in everything, that she let go of her father's hand for a moment, and wandered away. In just a few seconds she was lost.

The mother and father searched all over in the crowd for their daughter, and they notified the floor-walkers, they went to a policeman, they asked at the lost and found department, but she was nowhere to be found.

For several hours they hunted and wept.

A ten-year-old boy came to the father and said, "Mister, where is your little girl?"

The father said, "Son, I do not know. I wish somebody could find her."

Then the boy smiled and said, "Well, I found her and took her up to the lost and found department."

The father was so happy, so he said, "Where did you find her? Was she crying, and what did she say?"

The boy said, "Well, I saw all of you together in the toy department, several hours ago. Then, a few minutes ago, I was standing near the Van Buren Street entrance, and I saw the little girl start to go out of the door, and I knew she was lost. I asked her where she was going? She said, 'Outside.' 'Where is your father and mother?' I asked her. 'Oh,' she said, 'they're lost.' "

Yes, boys and girls, she said her father and mother were *lost*. She had not stopped to think that *she* was the one who was lost.

IS GOD LOST?

Many boys and girls have never found God, and they think God must be *lost*.

ADAM AND EVE LOST GOD

Ever since Adam and Eve sinned in the Garden of Eden, God has been lost to some people, but we must

CHANGE THE NAME OF THE LESSON

God is *not* lost—it is the *people* who are lost; so God sent His only Son down to "seek and to save that which was lost."

MAN WAS PERFECT

(Hold up Fig. 10.) Before man was lost, he was just like God—

perfect. (Pull cord back and forth, as in Fig. 10.) God made man in His own image. That means, they were just alike, or as one. They were friends, and often talked together, and visited in the Garden of Eden. There was no break between them. They were like this cord, united.

THEN CAME SORROW

One day sin came. (Hold up scissors, with SIN tag.) With sin comes sorrow. The Tempter whispered into the ear of Adam and Eve. They listened, and disobeyed God, and then this wonderful life of fellowship and friendship between man and God was broken. (Cut out the centre string. Fig. 4.)

SEPARATION FROM GOD

Any one can now see what happened. Man got separated from God. (Open object to Fig. 5.)

GOD'S WAY OF FINDING MAN

Once I lost a valuable part of my watch-chain. It was the emblem they gave me when I graduated from the seminary. I lost it in a strange city, and was there for only one day. I immediately planned to find it; so I went to the newspaper office and asked them to put a "lost" ad. in the paper. In a day or so, somebody returned it to me, for they had found it lying on the sidewalk.

God also made plans, when man got lost, to get him back.

THE FIRST PROMISE

He promised to send a Redeemer to save man. He was to be born of a woman, and He was to bruise the head of the serpent. The seed of the woman was Jesus, and the serpent was the devil.

THE FLOOD

God got the best man on earth, Noah, to warn the people about the Flood. The wicked people just laughed. After many years of warning, God sent the Flood, to cleanse the earth and give man a new start, leaving the eight best people surviving. Later, these eight also fell into ways of sin.

THE LAW

Then God sent the Law, but the people failed under this plan, too.

THE JUDGES

Then He sent the Judges, but the people despised the Judges and failed to come back to God under their rule.

THE KINGS

Then the people asked for a king; but they failed under the rule of the Kings, too.

THE PROPHETS

Then God sent them Prophets or Preachers, but the people laughed at their message, and stoned and killed them.

THE SAVIOUR WAS SENT

God still loved the people, and wanted them to come back to Him. Once more He showed His love to them, by sending His only Son JESUS, to die on the cross of calvary. Now He invites us to follow Him, and to bear a cross.

WE MUST HAVE FAITH

If you were lost in a woods and couldn't find your way out, and a man came along who knew the way out, and he offered to lead you out, you would follow him, would you not? You would forsake your way of wandering and go his way. That is what Jesus wants us to do. He wants us to say—what is on this card. (Hold up Fig. 6.)

"FORSAKING ALL, I TAKE HIM"

In order to take Jesus, we must give up all our sin. We can't have Jesus in our heart, and sin, too. If we want to be really happy Christians, we may have to throw some things out of our lives, even some big things.

GIVING UP OUR SIN

Let me take the biggest part of this paper, and tear it off and give it up or throw it away. (Cut as in Fig. 8.)

FAITH LEFT

Now see what I have left. I have FAITH. This is the biggest thing in the world. It may not look as big as what I have thrown away, but there is something hidden behind faith which makes it more valuable than anything in the whole world.

THE CROSS

(Show Fig. 9—the Cross.)

See, it is the SAVIOUR who is back of my faith. He says, "Greater love hath no man than this, that a man lay down his life for His friends." Jesus laid down His life to bring us back to God, when we were lost.

Don't you think that any one who would die on a cross for us, would also be willing to give us anything else we needed and asked for, if we have enough faith?

MAN WAS LOST, BUT CAN HE BE FOUND?

So far as God was concerned—man was lost. When sin came between man and God, it separated them, just as the string was cut and separated.

Now, how can we get back to God, so we can have fellowship and friendship with Him, and be one with Him again? Jesus must come between us and God. He must be like a bridge, with one hand on God, and the other hand on lost man, and then He can lift us up to God.

Let us apply our faith in Jesus the Saviour on the Cross to our broken lives, and see what happens.

(Touch the cross to the broken string, and close the pillars, and pull the string back and forth again.)

See, boys and girls, this is the way to get back to God, for by faith in the Saviour we, who were lost from God, can be united to Him and be as one with Him.

Are you lost in the woods? Listen to the voice of Jesus, for He says, as He leads you out, "Come unto Me—follow Me—I am the Way, the Truth and the Life."

76

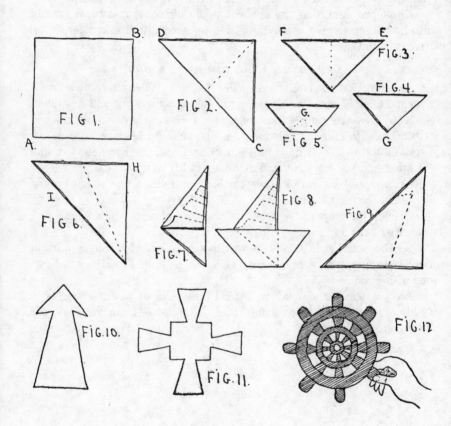

FIG 1.

FIG 2.

FIG.3.

FIG.4.

FIG 5.

FIG 6.

FIG.7.

FIG 8.

FIG 9.

FIG.10.

FIG.11.

FIG.12

XIII

ALL ABOARD FOR—SOMEWHERE

"Now my days are passed away as the swift ships."—JOB 9:25, 26.

MATERIAL NEEDED—

Paper and scissors.

CONSTRUCTION OF OBJECT—

Cut two pieces of paper, 14 inches square. Two colours would be effective, but one colour will do.

FIRST SQUARE

1. Take one square and fold Fig. 1, A to B, forming Fig. 2.

2. Fold Fig. 2, C to D, making Fig. 3.

3. Fold Fig. 3, E to F, making Fig. 4. Mark with a pencil, as in Fig. 9. When cut on these pencil-lines, and partly unfolded, the object should look like a lighthouse, as in Fig. 10.

4. Out of Fig. 4, make Fig 5, folding the corner G up. This will make it look like a crude boat.

SECOND SQUARE

1. Fold Fig. 1 through various steps to Fig. 4.

2. Note that Fig. 6 is the same as Fig. 4, except that the drawing is enlarged. Fold Fig. 6 or Fig. 4, H to I, and turn this upside down, as in Fig. 7.

3. Mark Fig. 7 with pencil-lines as shown. When this is cut and unfolded, it should look like a pilot-wheel, as in Fig. 12.

4. Put Fig. 7 in Fig. 5, so it looks like a common sailboat. See Fig. 8.

OBJECTS THAT RESULT FROM THE PAPER-FOLD

There are five steps to the Lesson, illustrated by the following objects, made from the paper-folds.

1. The plain boat. Fig. 5.

2. The sail on the boat. Fig. 8.

3. The lighthouse. Fig. 10.
4. The propeller. Fig. 11.
5. The pilot-wheel. Fig. 12.

Rehearse the folding and cutting thoroughly. Plan to fold the paper as you talk. If you cannot feel sure, prepare the folds beforehand, merely assembling in the meeting.

MUSIC SUGGESTIONS

Use seafaring songs, such as "Throw Out the Life-line," "Let the Lower Lights Be Burning," "Jesus, Saviour, Pilot Me."

THE LESSON

1. I want to talk about ships and boats. Ships were mentioned about fifty-six times in the Bible, and boats six times.

When our forefathers came from England, it took the boat, the *May-flower*, several months to cross the ocean. When David Livingstone sailed for Africa, it took the ship many weeks to get there. Today, however, ships cross the Atlantic Ocean in just a few days. The Bible tells us that our lives are like swift ships that soon pass out of sight. Soon after ships leave the harbour, they cannot be seen, for they travel fast. Life is short, and is indeed like the swift ships that soon pass out of sight.

(Hold up the boat. Fig. 5.) This looks like an old-fashioned row-boat. It would drift if put into the ocean alone, and soon be on the rocks. Boats starting on a voyage are bound for *somewhere,* but if a rowboat was started out like this, it would get *nowhere.*

I have never heard of any one going to Europe in a rowboat, at least I never heard of any one who *got* there that way. A boat, to make a successful voyage, must have more than a pair of oars, for it is just wood and has no sense; hence it would just drift.

Our lives must also have something more than just arms and legs, or we will drift, drift, drift, and get *nowhere.*

2. Most small boats have a SAIL. (Hold up Fig. 7 and make Fig. 8.)

The sails are put up, or hoisted, and when the wind blows the boat will move. Without sails, the boat would just drift. (If you can find a piece of driftwood, hold it up and state that this might have been a boat that drifted and was wrecked on the rocks.)

Many boys and girls are like a boat without sails. They drift with the tide, and get—nowhere. The tide is the crowd, the big thoughtless, pleasure-seeking, wicked crowd, that says, "Everybody come, all aboard, we are going—going—*nowhere*.

3. (Dismantle the ship and sail, and cut the LIGHTHOUSE out of Fig. 9, which is the boat part of Fig. 8.)

Many ships are lost at sea, even when they do have sails. They must have something to guide them to the harbour, so the government puts up lighthouses, near the harbour. Lighthouses are tall towers, with a great light in them, that can be seen for many miles at sea. The captain always steers a boat into the direction of the lighthouse. In the lighthouse there is also found a FOG-HORN. This horn sounds every minute when the weather is foggy, whether it be day or night. This guides the captain to the harbour, too. (Hold up Fig. 10.) This is what a lighthouse looks like.

Jesus is the Lighthouse to guide us on the sea of life. Unless we have Jesus as the light to guide us to the harbour, we may be wrecked in the sea of sin.

Just as the captain of a ship looks for the lighthouse, so we must "look unto Jesus, the Author and Finisher of our faith."

In our company, during the World War, certain men could not keep abreast in formation. These were formed into an "awkward squad." The corporal commanded them to watch a post on the far side of the field, and *not* to look to the right or left. When the men kept their eyes on the post, they kept a straight line. After they had learned this, they were put into the ranks of the company. Boys and girls, the sea-captain looks at the lighthouse, and the Christian must look at Jesus.

4. (Unfold the LIGHTHOUSE all the way, making Fig. 11.)

This is a propeller. Small boats use sails, but large ones use propellers. A propeller is on the rear end of the boat, and when it turns, the boat moves. The boats that are known as "sidewheelers" have a propeller or wheel on the side.

Great engines turn the propeller. This propeller has four blades, so I will name the four things that move the Christian in the right direction, in the sea of life.

Prayer—Bible study—attendance at Sunday School and church—Christian companionships.

These four things will move you along, even when the sea is rough and dangerous.

5. (Cut Fig. 7 on pencil-lines and make Fig. 12, when unfolded.)

This is the pilot-wheel. It is one of the most important parts of the ship. This wheel steers the ship. A ship may have sails or a propeller. It may be near the lighthouse, but unless it has a pilot-wheel, and a strong pilot to guide it, the ship will never reach the harbour. The pilot must know the dangerous places and be able to steer the ship away from these places. When a large ocean liner comes across the ocean, and it nears the New York Harbour, where great danger lurks, the captain sends out a signal, calling for a "harbour pilot." Then he stops the ship and waits. Soon a small boat comes towards the large boat, and a rope ladder is lowered. The harbour pilot, who knows the harbour and the tide, climbs up the ladder and he puts his hand upon the pilot-wheel, and this great pilot safely guides the ship to the harbour and dock.

Boys and girls, you are coming to a dangerous place in life. You are on the sea of life. You are bound for—somewhere. You need a pilot. You need Jesus. There are rocks, and shallow places. You are not safe without the Pilot, Jesus. Won't you let Him take the wheel of your life?

"Jesus, Saviour, pilot me,
    Over Life's tempestuous sea:
Unknown waves before me roll,
    Hiding rock and treacherous shoal;
Chart and compass come from Thee:
    Jesus, Saviour, pilot me.

"When at last I near the shore,
    And the fearful breakers roar
'Twixt me and the peaceful rest;
    Then, while leaning on Thy breast,
May I hear Thee say to me,
    'Fear not, I will pilot thee.'"

ADDITIONAL ILLUSTRATIONS

When Jesus took His journey from heaven to earth He had a round trip ticket. Earth was not His final destination. It was just a field of labour for a season.

But when we take the voyage of life we are not on a pleasure cruise with a round trip ticket. We are bound for a destiny that we will never leave, once we reach it, and we must pack our grips with that in mind.

Some one has said, "Many a man has a good aim in life, but he never pulls the trigger." Every mariner must decide his course.

The great Municipal pier that juts out into the Chicago Harbour is the place of decision for every sea Captain sailing Lake Michigan vessels.

When the great ship comes to that pier it has come to the end of the harbour, and then the Captain must decide which way to go. In the narrow harbour he can go only in one direction, but the end of that narrow course is the valley of decision, for, having come to the "big lake," he can go in many directions. The direction he chooses determines the destiny he will reach.

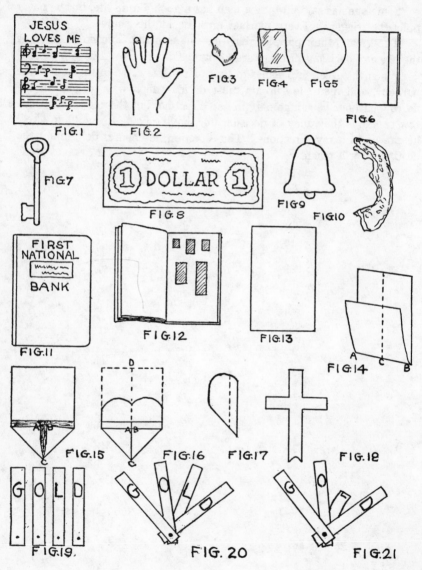

FIG.1   FIG.2   FIG.3   FIG.4   FIG.5   FIG.6

FIG.7   FIG.8   FIG.9   FIG.10

FIG.11   FIG.12   FIG.13   FIG.14

FIG.15   FIG.16   FIG.17   FIG.12

FIG.19   FIG.20   FIG.21

XIV

THE TWO MASTERS

"Choose you this day whom ye will serve."—Joshua 24:15.

MATERIAL NEEDED—

An old book.

A leaf from a hymn-book. (Preferably "Jesus Loves Me.")

A small stone.

A piece of broken glass.

A penny.

A razor-blade.

A door-key.

A dollar-bill.

A collapsible Christmas decoration-bell.

A crust of bread.

A bank-book.

Several pieces of white paper.

Cardboard.

Crayon or paints.

CONSTRUCTION OF THE OBJECT—

1. Paste hymn on inside cover of book.

2. Draw picture of a hand on a piece of paper, and place it between the leaves of the book.

3. With the razor-blade, cut holes through pages of book, large and deep enough to hold the stone and glass, the penny, the razor-blade and the key, as in Fig. 12. Hide these articles in the cut-outs.

4. Place the dollar-bill between the next uncut pages.

5. Cut more holes in the back pages of the book, and hide the collapsible bell, the bread-crust and the bank-book.

6. Get a piece of paper, 6 x 9 inches. Fold as in Fig. 14. Then fold corners, A and B, up as in Fig. 15. Fold on line, C to D, and cut as in Fig. 17, forming a heart. Place this between other pages of the book.

7. Make cardboard strips as in Fig. 20, holding them in fan shape with a paper-fastener. Print GOLD on them.

THE LESSON

A master is one who rules your life.

Today there are two masters who want to rule, and you must choose the one you want.

I want to show you what I mean by reading a story from this book. It will take five minutes to read this book through, so listen carefully.

Once there were two boys, brothers. They had the same mother, but they chose different masters. When they were quite small, the dear Christian mother taught them to sing that song you all know. (Show the song.)

> "Jesus loves me, this I know,
>   For the Bible tells me so,
> Little ones to Him belong,
>   They are weak, but He is strong.
> Yes, Jesus loves me!
> Yes, Jesus loves me!
> Yes, Jesus loves me!
>   The Bible tells me so!"

This mother was wise, for she wanted them to find Jesus as their Master.

THE FIRST BOY

The older boy made his choice of a master very early in life. He chose the wrong master, for he told lies, did wicked things, and learned to steal.

THE HAND

His hand got him into much trouble, for it took things that did not belong to him.

THE STONE

One day he picked up a stone. (Show STONE.) Most boys carry stones in their pockets, but this boy kept the stone in his hand, for he planned to use it.

THE GLASS

When the neighbours were not looking, he threw the stone at the window and broke the glass. (Show GLASS.) Then he ran away.

THE PENNY

Several days passed, and this boy planned to get his hand through the broken glass, to open the window and crawl in. One day he got in.

There were many valuable things in the house, such as trinkets, watches, jewels, and cookies and fruits. However, he wanted none of these. He was looking for money, pennies to spend. (Show PENNY.)

He found the baby's bank, and broke it open. Then this troublesome hand stuck the pennies into his pocket, and he crawled out of the window.

All of this he did because he chose the wrong master.

THE RAZOR-BLADE

How he grieved his mother's heart!

Soon he grew up, and became a young man, old enough to shave. (Show RAZOR-BLADE.)

THE KEY

When he got a little older, he got a number of keys that would fit most doors. These he wanted so he could get in to steal.

THE DOLLAR-BILL

Now he no longer cared to bother with pennies. He wanted dollars, and fives and tens.

THE BELL

One day the church-bell was ringing. Many years had passed now. There were many cars and people in front of the church. It was the funeral service for his mother. She had not seen him for many years, and she had worried about him so long, she had become ill, and grieved herself to death. They had sent for him to come to the funeral. He could not come, for he was in prison. *He had chosen the wrong master.*

THE SECOND BOY

Now let us look at the other boy, his brother. (Show the BELL.)

Every time the church-bell rang, this boy went to Sunday school and church. He, too, had chosen a Master, and each time he went to church he found his Master there.

THE CRUST

When he saw the poor, he helped them, sharing his clothes and money with them. He said, "When I help them, I am helping my Master."

He was willing to share his bread with the needy.   (Show CRUST.)

THE BANK-BOOK

This fine boy also got money.   Instead of stealing it, he earned it honestly.   He saved it and put it in the bank.   (Show BANK-BOOK.)

THE PREPARED PAPER HEART

He was happy and successful, because he had the right master in his heart.   (Show HEART.)

Now, who was this Master?   (Fold Fig. 17, and tear down the dotted line, making the cross.   Fig. 18.)

The Master of this boy's heart was Jesus, who died on the Cross, and who helps us to overcome temptation.   "Be of good cheer," He said, "for I have overcome the world."

THE GOLD

The boy who went to prison chose gold as his master.   (Show Fig. 20.) Gold ruled his life.   The Bible tells us that the root of all evil is the love for money.   I once saw a man hang on the gallows, because he had killed his landlady in order to get seventy-five cents from her.   This boy's master was *gold*.   (Turn the letter L down, as in Fig. 21.)

THE OTHER BOY'S MASTER WAS GOD

"Choose you this day whom ye will serve."

NOTE

The principle of hiding objects in a book was taught me by a drug addict who recently had been converted.   He had spent twenty-one years in prison.   After his conversion in a rescue mission, in Evansville, Indiana, I visited him in his shack on the Ohio River.   There he told me the story of his life, and how he had smuggled "dope" by cutting out certain sections of a book, and placing drugs and needles in their place.   His library was made up of mutilated books.

ADDITIONAL ILLUSTRATIONS

A helpful thought can be added to this lesson by showing the various "pockets" or holes in the book, after all the objects have been removed.

Then turn over a leaf of the book and cover the holes.   Ask if the holes are still in the book.   They are.

This symbolizes the folly of merely turning over a new leaf. It only covers that which went before, but does not obliterate it.

Hence with the scars of sin in our lives, just to begin all over again by turning over a new leaf is not enough. We must turn over a new leaf as far as the future is concerned, but we must accept Christ to take care of the past, for He says, "I will blot out as a thick cloud thy transgressions," and "thy sins and iniquities will I remember no more."

88

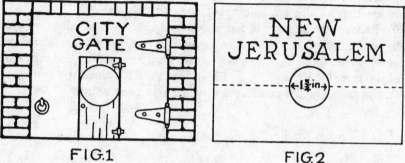

FIG.1

NEW
JERUSALEM
←1⅜in→

FIG.2

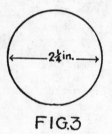

←2¼in.→

FIG.3

CITY

FIG.4

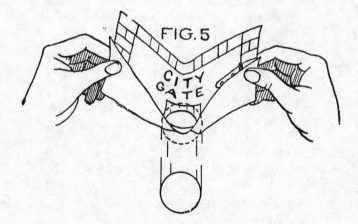

FIG.5

CITY
GATE

XV

A CAMEL THROUGH A NEEDLE'S EYE

"It is easier for a camel to go through the eye of a needle than for a rich man to enter into the kingdom of heaven."—MATTHEW 19:24.

MATERIALS NEEDED—

A piece of typewriting paper, 5½ x 8 inches.
Cardboard.
Crayon or paint.

CONSTRUCTION OF OBJECT—

1. On the typewriting paper, draw picture of a large gate. Fig. 1.
2. On one side of paper, print the words CITY-GATE, and on the other side NEW JERUSALEM. See Fig. 2.
3. Cut a disc from cardboard.
4. Cut out a circle from the small gate, making the circle about ½ inch smaller than the disc.

MANIPULATION

The idea of this Lesson is to put the large disc through the small hole, illustrating how the camel got through the eye of the needle. This is done by bisecting the hole with a crease, and laying the cardboard disc in the crease. Fig. 4. Then pull gently on the edges of the paper, upward and outward. Fig. 5. The disc will go through without tearing the paper or bending the disc.

THE LESSON

Jesus said (Matt. 19:24), "It is easier for a camel to go through the eye of a needle, than for a rich man to enter into the kingdom of heaven."

The needle's eye which Jesus had in mind was not the one of which you boys and girls are thinking. You have watched your mother patiently trying to put the thread through the eye of her needle. My, but it was difficult! Perhaps you tried to help her. This makes you imagine a camel could *never* get through. Watch and listen carefully, and I will show you how it was done.

In the first place, the needle's eye was not the eye of a sewing-needle. It was a small gate, built inside the large gate of the wall of an Eastern city. (Show picture.)

The large gate was built for heavy traffic, such as caravans of camels and oxen and carts. Sometimes, this gate was closed. It was never open on the Sabbath.

After the large gate was closed, people still went in and out of the city, but they used the small gate which was nicknamed "The Needle's Eye." It was just about the size of an ordinary door, and very small for a camel to get through.

Sometimes a man, coming from a long journey, late at night with a number of camels laden with perfumes and spices, would find the large gate closed, but the little one still open. Then he would set to work to get his camels through the small gate. Do you think he could do it?

SHOW THE LARGE DISC

Now note what I have. Here is the camel, and here is the needle's eye. The camel is much bigger than the hole in the gate, but I think I can get this camel through the gate, without tearing down the gate or breaking the camel's back. (Show how much larger the disc is than the hole.)

THE FREIGHT UNLOADED

Before the camel could get through, all the freight had to be unloaded.

Now let us put the camel through. (Crease the gate, bisecting the hole, and put the disc through, letting it fall down. Fig. 5.)

There! Now you see how a large camel could be gotten through the small needle's eye.

APPLICATION

Now, children, let us suppose the camel is one of us, and we must go through the narrow gate. We, too, must get rid of our load of freight. Each of us has a heavy load. It is not a load of spices and perfumes, but a load of black sin, and how heavy this load becomes as we grow older!

THE GATE OF HEAVEN

To enter the gate of heaven, we must leave the load of sin outside. Jesus bids us to cast all our care upon Him.

The camel had to get down upon his knees. He was too big to walk right through. We, too, must get humble before God, and get on our knees in prayer to God, if we would enter the gate of heaven.

On one occasion, the late Dr. A. C. Dixon took his boy to a large city. The boy saw men working on a tall building, and thought they were boys, because they looked so small. His father told him they were really men, but they looked so small because they were so high up. Then the boy said, "Well, Daddy, the closer they get to heaven, the smaller they get." How true!

The camel was interested in getting into *old* Jerusalem, but if we unload our sins and bow on our knees, we will enter the *new* Jerusalem, the heavenly city. (Turn the picture over and show these words.)

ILLUSTRATIONS

The Book of Hebrews says, "Let us lay aside every weight, and the sin which doth so easily beset us" (chap. 12:1). Unload your freight.

One night a man was seeking salvation in a rescue mission, but could find no peace. One of the workers noticed that he was kneeling, *but upon one knee only.* He said, "Get down on both knees," which meant full surrender. The camel had to get down on all-fours.

Charles Lindbergh flew across the Atlantic and reached his goal, chiefly because he took no companion or extra baggage with him. He was the "Lone Eagle." Commander Richard E. Byrd, although a great aviator and explorer, did not *quite* reach his goal. He had to come down in the water one hundred feet from shore. He had too heavy a load. He had taken provisions and a companion along. "Let us lay aside every weight."

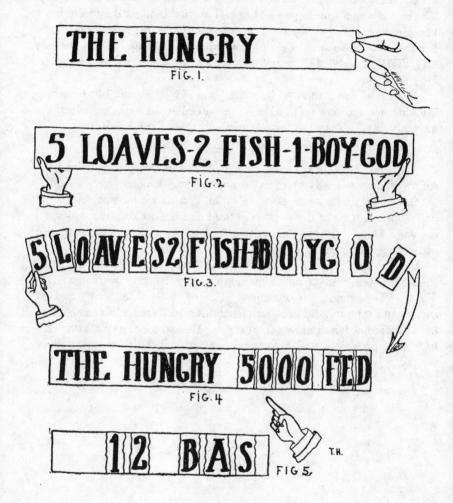

THE HUNGRY

FIG. 1.

5 LOAVES-2 FISH-1-BOY-GOD

FIG. 2

5 LOAVES 2 FISH 1 BOY GOD

FIG. 3.

THE HUNGRY 5000 FED

FIG. 4

12 BAS

FIG 5.

T.H.

XVI

A LITTLE BOY WITH A BIG HEART

The Feeding of the Five Thousand—JOHN 6:1-13.

MATERIAL NEEDED—

Cardboard.
Paper-clips.
Scissors.
Crayon or paint.

CONSTRUCTION OF OBJECT—

1. On a long piece of cardboard, print the words THE HUNGRY.
Leave a space at right hand end for further printing. Fig. 1.

2. On another piece of cardboard, print as in Fig. 2, the words—
5 LOAVES—2 FISH—1 BOY—GOD. Make these letters the same size as
in Fig. 1.

3. Have a shorter blank piece of cardboard in readiness for use in
the Lesson, to form Fig. 5.

THE LESSON

Jesus loves all children—but especially does He love little children,
with big, unselfish hearts.

One day a great crowd followed Jesus. His great heart was touched,
for He knew they were hungry, and so He began to plan to feed this
big crowd.

How would you like to feed five thousand people? If you have five
people in your family at home, Jesus had just one thousand times that
many to feed that day.

I want someone to help me, some little fellow with a big heart. Come
up here with me, and I will let you hold this card. (Give him the card—
THE HUNGRY.)

I will also need another little boy with a big heart. Who will come?
I will let you hold this card. (Give him the card—5 LOAVES—2 FISH—
1 BOY—GOD.)

Just as these two boys came to help me, so there was a little fellow who wanted to help Jesus. He was a little boy with a big heart. He went to the friends of Jesus and said, "I want to help Jesus all I can. I heard He was going to feed all this big crowd. I have a little lunch here; it is just five barley loaves [biscuits] and two small fish, but Jesus is welcome to them."

I imagine some of the disciples said, "Well, you had better keep some for yourself," and the boy replied, "No, I will give *all* I have to Jesus."

He was a boy with a big heart, was he not? How Jesus must have loved this boy, for being so unselfish as to give up *all* his lunch!

Now, let us see what happened.

First we see a big crowd of five thousand people. These we will call THE HUNGRY. (Point to this card.)

Second, we see 5 BARLEY LOAVES—2 FISH—1 BOY and JESUS, who was GOD. (Point to this card.)

Jesus told His friends to have the crowd to sit down on the grass. Then Jesus prayed, giving thanks to His Father for the five loaves and the two fish and the little boy with the big heart.

He began to break up the boy's lunch into pieces. Let us take the loaves and the fish apart, and see what happens. (Cut Fig. 2 up with the scissors, each letter separately, and put the letters in place, back of THE HUNGRY, fastening with paper-clips.)

First we will break off the 5. Then the o, and now another o, and also the last o. (Put these all in place, making 5000. Fig. 4.)

We also will break off the F and the E and the D. (Place these as in Fig. 4.)

Ah, see what has happened. Because this little boy with the big heart gave his lunch to Jesus, THE HUNGRY 5000 WERE FED.

Let us look again. The Bible tells us that Jesus broke up all the bread and fish. (Cut apart the remaining twelve letters.)

Jesus had twelve friends, who also helped Him. He never forgets those who help Him. He called these friends "disciples." When all of these five thousand were fed, Jesus told His disciples to gather up the pieces that were left over. They gathered twelve baskets full. (Count out the twelve letters you have in your hand.)

Twelve baskets full, one for each disciple. (Out of the twelve letters, select these—

12-B-A-S

(Clip these in place on the blank card. Fig. 5.)

Each disciple wore a girdle, or belt, and it is thought that there was a pocket, arranged for food to be carried in this belt, and that the basket here mentioned was enough to fill this belt-pocket. This was likely just about enough for one meal.

Boys and girls, I have often wondered what Jesus did for the little boy with the big heart. I think, that after the five thousand hungry people were fed, and the disciples each had a basket of food, Jesus took this boy to one side and said, "My boy, what did you give?" The boy said, "Why, I gave five loaves and two fish."

Then Jesus said, "Yes, and with those loaves and fish, I fed five thousand hungry people, and I gave each of my friends a basketfull of food. Now I want to give you back what you gave. Here are the two fish. (You will have seven cards in your hand. Hold up two of them, and hand them to one of the boys.) And here are the five loaves." (Hand the remaining five cards to the boy.)

And so, this little boy with the big heart lost nothing by being unselfish, for not only did he help feed five thousand hungry people and supply the twelve disciples each with a basket, but he was fed by Jesus and still had all that he started with, for

HE GOT BACK ALL THAT HE GAVE.

96

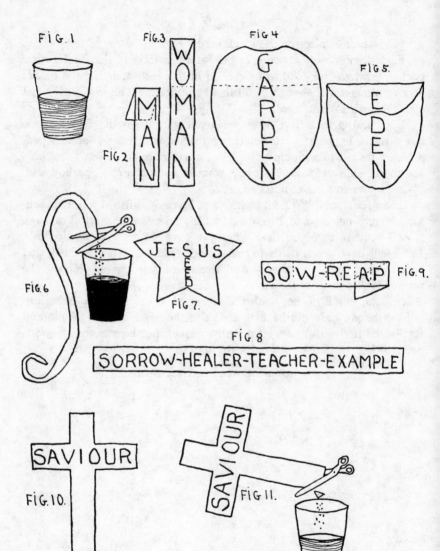

FIG. 1

FIG. 3 — WOMAN

FIG. 2 — MAN

FIG 4 — GARDEN

FIG 5. — EDEN

FIG. 6

FIG. 7. — JESUS / SEED

FIG. 9. — SOW-REAP

FIG. 8

SORROW-HEALER-TEACHER-EXAMPLE

FIG. 10. — SAVIOUR

FIG 11. — SAVIOUR

XVII

THE WORLD'S BIGGEST GARDEN SOLD FOR A SIN

"Whatsoever a man soweth, that shall he also reap."—GALATIANS 6:7.

MATERIAL NEEDED—

Scissors, glass of water, wooden pencil for stirring, cardboard, wrapping paper, crayon or paints, paper clips, glue.

Fifteen cents' worth of chemicals. (Oxalic acid, 5 cents; tannic acid, 5 cents; tincture of iron, 5 cents.)

CONSTRUCTION OF OBJECT—

1. Put four drops of tincture of iron into a glass.

2. Make Figs. 2 and 3 out of cardboard. Fig. 2 is Fig. 3 with the w o folded back.

3. Make Figs. 4 and 5 from cardboard. Fig. 5 is Fig. 4 with top folded forward and down. The letter E is printed on back of Fig. 4. When folded down, it covers GAR.

4. Make Fig. 6 out of cardboard. Make a small packet or envelope to hold about 4 pinches of tannic acid. Paste this packet on back of snake head, so that when it is cut, the tannic acid will fall into glass. This will turn the water black, when you stir, to mix with tincture of iron.

5. Cut out star and print as in Fig. 7.

6. Print the words—SORROW—HEALER—TEACHER—EXAMPLE, on a long strip of wrapping-paper. Fig. 8.

7. Fold letters of Fig. 8 out of way, so only SOW—REAP shows. Hold this position with paper-clips. Fig. 9.

8. Make a cross, Fig. 10, and print SAVIOUR on it.

9. Make packet to hold 4 pinches of oxalic acid, and paste packet on back of bottom of cross, so it can be cut open, as in Fig. 11.

THE LESSON

PLAYING GARDEN

Did you ever play garden? You have played store and school and church, I suppose. Somebody always wants to be teacher, or storekeeper, or minister. I hope some of you will grow up into these.

PLAYING TABERNACLE

Evangelist George T. Stephens held many great evangelistic campaigns over the country in a large tabernacle. On one occasion he held a meeting in a town, and some months later he went to visit in that town. A mother told him that the children liked to play "Tabernacle" since he left. She said one of the children wanted to be George Stephens, the evangelist. Another wanted to be the song-leader. Another the pianist, and another the janitor. There was an extra boy one day, and there seemed to be no job for him to play.

The children said, "What are you going to be in the Tabernacle?" He puckered up his mouth and angrily said, "I am going to be the devil."

We are going to play garden, but this garden already had the devil in it, so I won't need anybody to play that part.

A GARDEN THAT HAD NO SEED PLANTED IN IT

There were large, beautiful trees and flowers and vegetables, and much fruit in this garden, and yet no one had ever planted any seed in it.

EDEN THE PLACE OF DELIGHT

1. (Hold up Fig. 4, representing fruit.)

God gave this garden a name. He called it Eden. (Fold top of GAR-DEN down, as in Fig. 5.)

Eden means "delight," for it was truly a place of delight and pleasure. No sin had ever entered there. There were animals in this garden,

BUT THESE ANIMALS DID NOT BITE

None of the animals were fierce or dangerous. They all lived together like a happy family. A lion was never heard to roar, and a tiger was never known to bite.

THE FIRST PEOPLE

2. Then God made man, so he could enjoy all of these things. (Hold up Fig. 2.) This man was Adam. He was the first and only man at this time. He must have been lonesome, so God made another person.

He took a part of this man, his rib, and made a woman, so the wife has always been close to the husband's heart. (Hold up Fig. 3.) Billy Sunday has said that "Woman is an improved edition of man."

God called this woman Eve, which means "the mother of all living," for Eve was the first mother. You will notice from this card that MAN AND WOMAN are as one. (Manipulate the card to show this.) God said they were to be as one.

THE BREATH OF LIFE

3. After God made man's body, He gave him life. He breathed into his nostrils the breath of life. (Pour the glass half-full of water. The glass should have the tincture of iron in it.)

This water represents the pure life God gave to Adam, for God made him in His own image or likeness.

SOWING AND REAPING

4. You will remember we are playing garden. God says, "Whatsoever a man soweth, that shall he also reap" (Gal. 6:7). In other words, when we have a garden, if we sow radish seed, we will get radishes. If we sow wheat, we will reap wheat.

SIN—SORROW—DEATH

There is a seed that brings forth a harvest of sorrow and death. That seed is DISOBEDIENCE TO GOD.

If we sow disobedience, which separates us from God, we will reap sorrow and death.

THE FIRST SIN

This was the seed the first man and woman, Adam and Eve, sowed. They disobeyed God. God said they could eat the fruit, in the garden, from all the trees but one. God was good to give them everything in the garden but one tree.

They often looked at that tree and wanted just a taste of it. Soon they said, "What will be the difference? Maybe if we do taste it, God will never know." *That was the devil in the garden.*

One day, while Eve was standing before the tree, wishing she could taste the fruit, a beautiful serpent came. Yes, a *beautiful* serpent. Some wonder if a snake could be beautiful. Remember I told you the animals lived like a big family, peacefully in the garden, then. None of them ever roared or clawed or bit, and even the snakes were beautiful. They did not even crawl on their stomachs then, but walked uprightly, in a rolling fashion, like this. (Show Fig. 6.)

THE DEVIL—SATAN

Now Satan, the devil, the father of sin, spoke through this serpent. Note that the serpent looks like a big letter s. That stands for

SERPENT—SATAN—SIN

He told Eve that she would not die, if she ate of this tree, but that she would become as wise as God.

THE PURE LIFE LOST

5. She listened to the voice of the serpent, the devil, and she sowed the seed of disobedience, through the mouth of the serpent—the devil, the deceiver. (Cut open the packet of tannic acid, and let it fall into the water. Then stir with pencil. Fig. 6.)

My, oh, my! See what has happened to the pure life! It has become blackened with sin. This is the harvest of the seed of disobedience, "For whatsoever a man soweth, that shall he also reap."

Eve ate of the forbidden fruit, and gave some to Adam, and from that moment they began to pay the price for their sin, and that price was:

1. They were sentenced to death.
2. They were expelled from the beautiful garden.
3. Adam had to earn his bread by the sweat of his brow.
4. Eve had to suffer much pain and sorrow as a mother.
5. The ground was cursed with thorns.
6. The serpent was made to crawl on his stomach for ever.

This was the harvest of the seed they had sown in the garden. How sad Eve must have been when God gave her two sons, Cain and Abel, and one of them killed the other. This was the result of her own sin of disobedience. She was reaping what she sowed.

6. However, God loved them. He loves all sinners. He arranged plans to save them for heaven, since they were to die from earth.

He promised another seed, for the garden. He called it the Seed of the Woman. This seed was Jesus. Later He became known as the Seed of David. He came to bruise the serpent's head, and to destroy the works of the devil (Gal. 3:15). (Hold up the star.)

THE COMING OF JESUS—THE SEED OF SALVATION

The prophets told about Jesus coming. Many years later He was born in Bethlehem. Wise men from the East came to worship Him, and a great star led them to the Seed of the Woman.

JESUS FOUND PEOPLE REAPING AS THEY SOWED

7. There was great sorrow in the world after sin came. Even the animals began to roar and snap and bite. The world was lost, but God loved it, so He sent His only Son to save it. Wherever Jesus went, He saw sorrow, the harvest of sin. He saw the truth of the saying, "Whatsoever a man soweth, that shall he also reap." (Hold up Fig. 9.)

NO SALVATION WITHOUT A SAVIOUR

8. (Open up Fig. 9 to Fig. 8.)

Jesus came to bear the sorrow of the people. He was a great HEALER. He healed the lame and the sick, and He gave eyes to the blind.

He was also a great TEACHER. He stood on the mountain-side, and by the seashore, and taught the people about God and heaven.

Jesus was a wonderful man, for He was always tender and helpful. He never sinned, so He was a wonderful EXAMPLE. Oh, if we could only be like Jesus! But I'm afraid we can't.

JESUS THE ONLY SAVIOUR

9. Jesus was more than a Healer and Teacher and Example. He came to be our Saviour, to save us from our sins. He had to live, in order to heal and to teach and to be an example; but to save us, He had to die.

"I came not to be ministered unto, but to minister, and to give my life a ransom for many."

HOLD UP THE CROSS

Jesus died on the Cross, and when He did this He planted new seed in the great garden. On the Cross He bruised the head of the serpent, and it was here He planted the seed of salvation, which will bring eternal life to those who believe (John 3:16). "For God so loved the world, etc."

THE CHANGED LIFE

10. The only way we can have this old, black, sinful life made clean is to come to Jesus, at the foot of the Cross, confessing our sins.

(Cut open the packet of oxalic acid, Fig. 11, and let the acid fall into the water. Stir with the pencil. This should clear up the water. If it does not, you have not used enough oxalic acid.)

See what happens when we do this. God can't see our sins through the Cross.

FIG 1.

FIG 2

FIG. 3.

FIG 4.

XVIII

THE LATEST NEWS *

(For the Week Preceding Rally Day)

MATERIAL NEEDED—

A piece of white wrapping-paper.
Black crayon or paint.

CONSTRUCTION OF OBJECT—

Upon a piece of white wrapping-paper, 6 x 36 inches, print the words

NEXT SUNDAY IS RALLY DAY

Fold the strip as illustrated in Figs. 2 and 3, so only the word EXTRA can be seen. Fasten this position with a paper-clip.

THE LESSON

You have all heard about Col. Charles Lindbergh. He is known as "The Lone Eagle," because he piloted his plane across the Atlantic Ocean alone. He has also been called "Lucky Lindy," because he has been successful in avoiding accidents.

His first son was known as "the eaglet," which means "Little Eagle," for everybody expected he, too, would be a flier. However, this did not happen, for one morning newsboys were all over in every neighbourhood, in every town and village, shouting at the top of their voices, "Extra! Extra!"

Why? Because somebody had crept into the Lindbergh home the night before, and had stolen the "eaglet" from his crib. The baby of "The Lone Eagle" had been kidnaped.

The whole country was deeply stirred, because everybody had learned to love Colonel and Mrs. Lindbergh, and the little "eaglet."

Many anxious weeks passed. The newspapers printed everything they could find out about the baby. When any new facts were learned,

---

* First published in *Church Management*.

they immediately sent out "extras," in order to give the people the latest news.

Many city officials said that when the baby was found, all the whistles in the city, and the bells in the churches would be heard. This was to be the sign that the baby had been found. For many days the parents and the people waited for the good news.

So far as we know, no whistle ever blew and no church-bell rang when the baby eaglet was found—because *it was dead*. This was the latest news, but it was bad news.

All over the cities and towns and villages, the boys were again crying, "Extra! Extra! Extra! Extra!"

Perhaps you noticed that I have an EXTRA here. I want to give you the latest news. Some of you have been away on vacations, and away from church and Bible school and home. Perhaps you have not heard the latest news.

A very important event is going to take place very soon. There will be a lot of enthusiasm and a big crowd. It will be for young and old, for friends and strangers, for relatives, fathers, mothers, aunts, uncles, cousins, brothers, sisters—in fact, the whole town is invited.

So important is this event that the Bible school superintendent decided we had to have an EXTRA out for it, so all the people would know the latest news.

When this event takes place, even the church-bells will ring.

I am not a newsboy, but I am shouting "Extra! Extra!"

Let us open up this EXTRA and see what the latest news is.

Our newsboy rides a bicycle, and he folds the paper up neatly, and tosses it on the porch, as he rides by. Then I get it, and unfold it and read the latest news. (Unfold the strip.)

NEXT SUNDAY IS RALLY DAY

NOTE—This can also be used for Children's Day, for the word EXTRA will work out in the same way.

ADDITIONAL ILLUSTRATIONS

To further illustrate how the children can get a big attendance, cut a long strip of paper and fold it in accordion pleat fashion.

Then draw a dim outline of a boy or girl and, at the proper time, cut out the shape as drawn. Be sure the arms extend to the edge of paper, so all arms will be joined together.

The result, when unfolded, will be a long string of boys or girls holding hands. This will encourage the children to bring others with them for the Rally Day services.

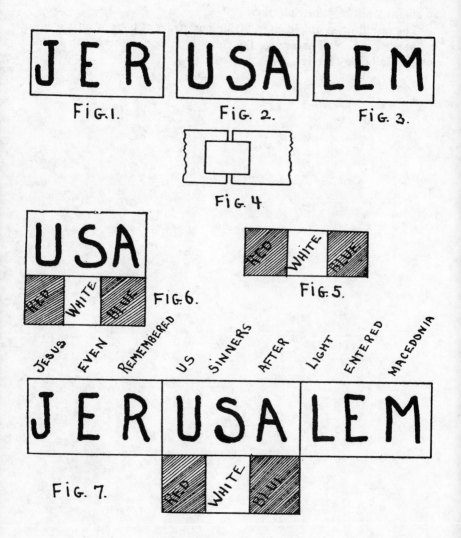

JER

Fig. 1.

USA

Fig. 2.

LEM

Fig. 3.

Fig. 4

USA
RED WHITE BLUE
Fig. 6.

RED WHITE BLUE
Fig. 5.

Jesus Even Remembered Us Sinners After Light Entered Macedonia

JER USA LEM

Fig. 7.

RED WHITE BLUE

XIX

SETTING THE WHOLE WORLD ON FIRE

(A Missionary Lesson)

MATERIAL NEEDED—

Cardboard.

Crayon or paint.

Gummed paper, or paper and glue.

CONSTRUCTION OF OBJECT—

1. Print the word JERUSALEM on a piece of cardboard, 2½ x 9 inches.
2. Cut into three parts. Figs. 1, 2, 3.
3. Cut another cardboard, the same width and a little shorter than the U S A piece. Fig. 2.
4. Colour this piece with red, white, blue. Fig. 5.
5. Hinge Figs. 1, 2, 3, together with tape as in Figs. 4 and 7.
6. Hinge Fig. 5 to U S A, Fig. 6. Fold it up and back of U S A.

THE LESSON

A BIG FIRE

When I was a boy, in Michigan City, Indiana, a great fire broke out in the Haskell and Barker Car Company's lumber-yard.

All the fire departments from surrounding towns were called. The heat was so intense that the firemen could not get near enough to put water on the fire, with their hose. My, but it was a fire! It was the kind a boy likes to go to.

It was reported that the whole city was burning to ashes. After many hours of fire-fighting, somebody told the chief to send to the Aetna Powder Mills, and get dynamite to throw into the fire to scatter it, so the heat would not be so intense. This would enable the firemen to get near it with their fire-hose.

A truck was sent to get the dynamite from the mills, twenty miles away.

THE BIG EXPLOSION

Everybody was sent away. Then the dynamite was thrown into the fire. The explosion was terrific. Fire shot high into the air, and great piles of lumber tottered and fell in a heap. Flaming boards went in all directions.

THE WHOLE CITY WAS SET ON FIRE

In just a few minutes calls came from all over the city for help. Grass patches, garages, stores, houses, schools, everything seemed to be on fire. The dynamite had scattered the big fire all over the city. Truly, the whole city was on fire!

THE GOSPEL-FIRE

Now I read in my Bible about a great fire. This fire was so great that it set many other places on fire, and if it keeps on, it will set the whole world on fire. It is the Gospel-fire.

We have a missionary lesson today. Jesus was the first missionary of the New Testament days.

He left His home in heaven, and came as a missionary to earth to save the whole world.

Jesus was born in Bethlehem, but He did most of His work in and around a town, the name of which I have here. (Hold up JERUSALEM, with red, white and blue folded out of sight.)

A GREAT RELIGIOUS CENTRE

Jerusalem was in the land of Palestine, and it was a great religious centre. There were over four hundred churches, which were called synagogues, in that city.

Now Jesus came to teach the people the whole truth about God, and to show Himself as the promised Messiah. But Jerusalem persecuted Jesus and planned to crucify Him. Before He was crucified, He got a few followers, to whom He gave the gospel. In this little band, the greatest fire in all the world was started. In just one day, through the preaching of just one man, over three thousand people were won to Jesus. These people formed the first Church.

THE CHRISTIANS WERE KILLED

This new Church made the Jews angry. They stoned the Christians and put them into prison.   Many were driven from place to place, and many were killed.   Even Stephen, the first deacon, was killed with stones.

Then the Christians decided they would run away for their lives, and this was what set the whole world on fire.

The Jews planned to put out this Gospel Fire by driving the Christians out, but when the Christians ran away from Jerusalem, they took the Gospel with them, so it was like the dynamite in the big fire.   Instead of putting out the big fire, little fires were started all over, and wherever the Christians went, new churches were started.

THE GOSPEL JUMPED ACROSS THE SEA

From Jerusalem, the Gospel was carried to Asia Minor.   A few years passed, and then a great man named Saul was converted.   He was one of the Jews who had driven the Christians out and had thrown them into prison.   After he was converted his name was changed to Paul.

One night Paul was standing on the seashore in a town named Troas. As he listened to the waves, he prayed.   As he prayed, he looked into the heavens, and there before him stood a man, a foreign man, a Macedonian. The man said, as he reached out his hands toward Paul,

"COME OVER INTO MACEDONIA AND HELP US"

Macedonia was across the Ægean Sea, and Paul decided the people needed the Gospel there, too, so he left Asia Minor and crossed the sea and went to Macedonia, which was a part of Europe.   This brought the Gospel much closer to our land.

Paul had no churches to preach in, so he went to the seaside in the open air and preached.   There he secured converts, and soon there were churches all over this land, too.

AMERICA WAS NOT YET DISCOVERED

At this time America had not yet been discovered, for it was about fourteen hundred years before Christopher Columbus lived.

THE FIRE IS BROUGHT OVER TO AMERICA

After the Gospel came to Europe, America was discovered, and the Gospel-fire took another jump.   This time it jumped clear across the Atlantic Ocean, from England, and it came to the good old U S A, which stands for the United States of America.   (Here fold back the JER and the LEM.)

THE NATIONAL COLOURS

The colours found in our flag are red, white, and blue. (Unfold coloured card.)

These colours stand for something, too.   When the Gospel came here it spread the glad news that Jesus had shed His blood for us on the Cross of Calvary.   RED stands for the blood that Jesus shed.

WHITE stands for the cleansing that blood gave us, so we could be white in our hearts.

BLUE stands for heaven, for if we follow Jesus we will go to heaven.

You know, if we had no churches in our land, our flag would be RED. It would stand for murder and blood.   We would be savages and perhaps cannibals.   I am glad Paul saw that vision that night, and brought the Gospel from Asia Minor to Macedonia in Europe, and then to the U S A.

JESUS EVEN REMEMBERED US SINNERS AFTER LIGHT ENTERED MACEDONIA

I would like to teach you one more lesson.   (Unfold the entire word JERUSALEM.)   Each one of these letters stands for a word, and we will say them together in a moment.   Here they are:

J stands for JESUS.   E stands for EVEN.   R stands for REMEMBERED, etc.

Here is the whole sentence.

J esus
E ven
R emembered
U s
S inners
A fter
L ight
E ntered
M acedonia.

Let us all say it together, as I point to the letters.
Now let us go back and trace the Gospel.

It came from HEAVEN;
Then to JERUSALEM;
Then to ASIA MINOR;
Then to MACEDONIA IN EUROPE;

> Then to NORTH AMERICA;
> Then to the U S A.

And now we are sending it out to all parts of the world, through our missionaries, and soon the whole world will be set on fire with the love of Jesus.

Remember Jesus said, *"Go ye into all the world, and preach the Gospel to every creature."*

112

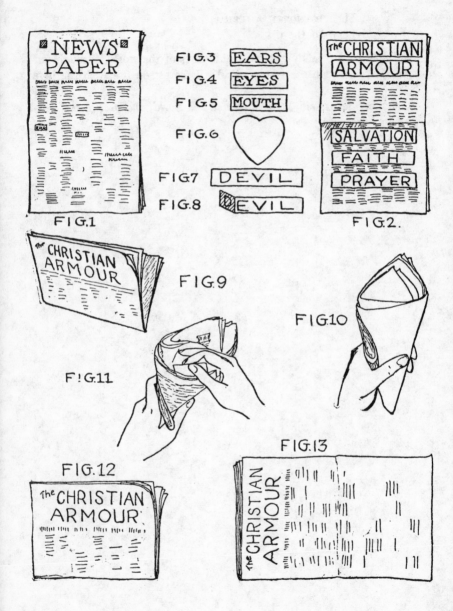

XX

THE CHRISTIAN ARMOUR

(Suitable for any season, but especially good for Armistice Sunday,
Independence Sunday or Decoration Day)
Scripture Lesson—EPHESIANS 6:11-18.

MATERIAL NEEDED—

One newspaper with a number of sheets.
White paper.
Cardboard.
Glue.
Crayon or paint.

CONSTRUCTION OF OBJECT—

1. Secure a newspaper.
2. On pieces of white paper, print THE CHRISTIAN ARMOUR. Glue this on the newspaper. Fig. 2.
3. On another slip of paper, print

> TRUTH
> RIGHTEOUSNESS
> PEACE
> FAITH
> SALVATION
> GOD'S WORD
> PRAYER.

Paste these on the newspaper beforehand. Fig. 2.
4. Upon smaller pieces of paper, print

> EARS
> EYES
> MOUTH
> DEVIL.

(Figs. 3, 4, 5, 7.)
5. Fold D of DEVIL back of E, spelling EVIL. Fig. 8.
6. Cut out a cardboard heart, not too large. Fig. 6.

113

THE LESSON

We hope there will never be another war. The last terrible war ended before you were born, and as long as you live I hope there will never be another. Nothing pleases Satan more than to see men killing one another. Did you know that during the last 3,421 years of the world's history, there have been 3,153 years of war? Only 268 years have been peaceful.

THE CHRISTIAN ARMOUR

When we live the Christian life, we are soldiers of the Cross, and there are apt to be great dangers. Our greatest enemy, the devil, will send his armies against us. He will use his weapons against us to destroy us. God has a plan whereby we will be protected. He gives us an armour to wear. An armour is like an iron suit.

THE DUCK'S ARMOUR

Did you ever see a duck swim in water? No matter how long it stays in the water, it never gets wet. This is because God gave it an armour to wear, to protect it from the water.

A certain oil comes out of the duck's body and feathers and keeps the duck dry, and that is the reason we often say, "It was like water running off a duck's back."

THE BEAR'S ARMOUR

In the mountains of the North, where there is snow all the year round, and where it is very cold, the bears live. Boys and girls couldn't live there, because they would soon freeze to death. The bears don't freeze, because God gave them an armour of fur to protect them from the cold.

THE DIVER'S ARMOUR

When I was a boy, I went out to the piers of Lake Michigan, and I saw a diver. He had a rubber suit on, and a great metal helmet. His shoes had iron soles. This made his feet heavy, so he could stay on the bottom of the lake.

I saw him stand on the side of a boat, and then he purposely fell over backwards into the water. Down, down, down he went, and the bubbles came up!

Fastened to him was a rope. This he used to give signals to the men on the boat, for they held one end of the rope. On his helmet there was a rubber hose, with flexible steel around it. This was fastened to a hand pump, and through it they sent air for him to breathe, while he was under the water.

He worked under the pier for a half-hour, and then he gave them the signal to pull him up. They pulled, and pulled, and pulled. Soon they had him out of the water. He was wet only on the outside. When he took his helmet and rubber suit off, he was perfectly dry. The diver's armour had protected him from the water.

AN ARMOUR FOR BOYS AND GIRLS

Now to the Christian armour. We are living in a very wicked world. All around us are temptations, but we must not give up to these temptations.

Martin Luther said, "We can't help it if the birds fly around our heads, but we can help it if they build nests in our hair."

THE NEWSPAPER

(Hold up newspaper, with CHRISTIAN ARMOUR on it. Fig. 2.)

THE PARTS OF THE ARMOUR

The ancient soldier wore an iron armour to protect him from the bullets and arrows of the enemy. The armour had a breastplate for the breast, and iron fittings for the feet. It had a shield which was carried in the hand. There was a helmet for the head. The soldier also had a sword. The Christian armour has all of those parts, too. The armour is made up of

> TRUTH
> RIGHTEOUSNESS
> PEACE
> FAITH
> SALVATION
> GOD'S WORD
> PRAYER.

(Point to all of these.)

OUR WORST ENEMY

Our worst enemy tries to get us to do evil. (Show EVIL.) He is the devil. (Show the D on EVIL.)

THE ARMOUR PROTECTS US

(Roll the paper into a cone, as in Fig. 10. Make a new opening in the cone by punching your hand down between the leaves, pushing the extra leaves back and leaving but two or three in place. See Fig. 11. Study this part carefully, and experiment.)

The devil would like to have our ears. (Hold up EARS.) We must put these ears into the armour. (Place EARS into the new opening of cone.) Now the devil can't whisper to us. Whenever we listen to bad words, lies, evil stories, etc., the devil has our ears.

EYES

The devil also wants our eyes. How he deceives the eyes! He deceived Eve in the Garden of Eden. She looked at the fruit, and her eyes told her it was good, so she let the devil have her eyes and she sinned against God. We must put our eyes into the armour, to hide them away from the devil. (Put EYES in.)

THE MOUTH

Satan also wants the mouth of every boy and girl. He wants us to speak sharply and unkindly. He wants us to be sassy to our parents, and to take God's name in vain. He wants us to tell lies, and to lose our tempers and to say mean things. So we must put the mouth into the armour, too, to protect it from the devil. (Put MOUTH in.)

THE HEART

And here is the heart. Above all things, Satan would like to have the heart. If he can get the heart, he knows he will get the ears, eyes, mouth, and the hands and feet. We must put the heart into the armour. (Put HEART in.)

Now that all these are safe in the armour, we need not be afraid, for we are protected by truth, righteousness, peace, faith, salvation, God's word, prayer.

THE DEVIL MUST FAIL

When we have such an armour, the devil must fail, for we are beyond his reach. He has a great army, made up of slaves whom he captured, while they were not in the Christian armour. He has a lot of boys and girls in this army, too, but we won't help him, will we? We will hide in the Christian armour.

WE ARE REALLY HIDDEN

Let us see if the devil can find us. (Show DEVIL again, and put it into the opening, taking it out again. Do this several times. As you do this, say, "He can't find the eyes, nor the ears, nor the mouth, for they are hidden in the armour.")

(Unfold the paper to Fig. 12.)

The devil has failed, for truly we are hidden and he can't find us.

(It will appear that the slips are in the other fold of the paper, and the children may suggest that you open the paper to position of Fig. 13. Hesitate to do this, as if you are afraid. After you have appeared worried, open it up to Fig. 13, being careful that the hinge is on the bottom. If the children insist on further opening, simply shake out the slips and say that God does not destroy our ears or eyes or mouth or heart, He just hides them in the Christian armour, for he said (Rom. 12:1), "I beseech you therefore . . . that ye *present* your bodies a living sacrifice, *holy* and acceptable unto God, which is your reasonable service.")

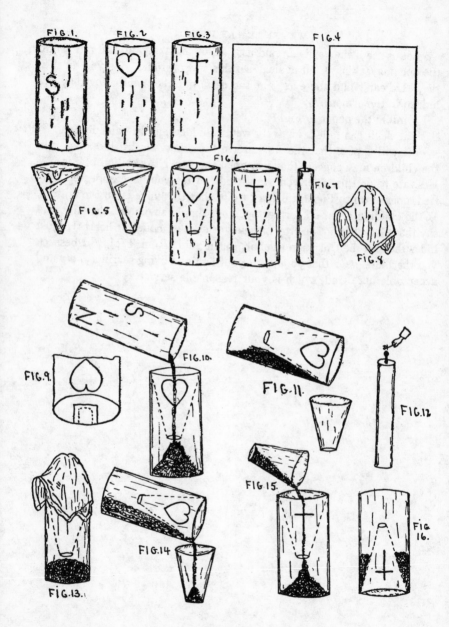

FIG.1. FIG.2 FIG.3 FIG.4

FIG.5 FIG.6 FIG.7 FIG.8.

FIG.9. FIG.10. FIG.11. FIG.12

FIG.13. FIG.14 FIG.15. FIG.16.

XXI

CAUGHT WITH THE GOODS

Joshua—Chap. 7.

MATERIAL NEEDED—

Three round salt or Quaker Oats boxes.

Salt.

Light-weight cardboard.

A candle and match.

A handkerchief.

A glass.

Gummed paper, or paper and glue.

Crayon or paint.

CONSTRUCTION OF OBJECT—

1. Cover the three boxes with gummed paper, or paper and glue, for neatness.

2. Take two pieces of light-weight cardboard, Fig. 4, and make two cones like Fig. 5. Hold these in shape with glue.

3. Cut out a piece from the top of one of the cones, after you have fitted it to one of the boxes. See Fig. 5 at A.

4. Place the two cones in two of the boxes, as in Fig. 6. Seal these in place.

5. Draw a heart on the box with the cut-out at A. Draw a Cross on other box.

6. Paste a piece of gummed paper over the cut-out in the heart cone, as in Fig. 9. Mark this place, so you can locate it later.

7. Print SIN on the third box, Fig. 1, and pour a cupful of salt into the box.

THE LESSON

I have a story to tell about two men, two cities, a Sunday suit, some silver coins, a bar of gold, and a tent. It is a true story from the history of Israel.

119

THE FALL OF JERICHO

The army of Israel had captured Jericho. All about the streets lay the spoils. God had placed a curse over the city, and He told Joshua, the commander of the army, that no one was to be allowed to take any of the spoils, or the curse would come into their camp and army.

ACHAN—A GOOD SOLDIER

In the camp, living in a soldier's tent, was a man named Achan. One day Achan walked through the streets of old Jericho. Lying on the street was a beautiful Sunday suit, a Babylonish garment. All the best cloth and goods came from Babylonia. This garment was highly coloured and beautiful.

ACHAN STOLE THE ROBE

(Hold up Fig. 1—SIN—the box with the salt in it. Also Fig. 2, the box with the heart on it.)

Achan saw nobody around, and he wanted the suit. Quickly he rolled it up and placed it under his coat and ran to his tent with it.

That was sin, so we will put SIN in the heart of Achan. (Pour some salt from sin-box into heart-box.)

HE BURIED THE ROBE IN HIS TENT

(Pick up handkerchief and cover box.)

This handkerchief represents the tent. Achan dug a hole in the ground, under the tent, and hid the robe in it.

THE SILVER SHEKELS

Soon Achan went out of his tent again. He was worried and frightened. Perhaps someone had seen him steal. Something in his heart was very heavy and sad.

Suddenly he came upon another sight. Lying at his very feet was a huge pile of silver coins—perhaps a hundred dollars or more—right on the street. It had been dropped there during the warfare against the city. No one had dared touch it, for fear of the curse.

Well, Achan decided that if he could hide a robe, he could hide the money, too.

Quickly grabbing it up, he ran to his tent with the money. This was another great sin, for he disobeyed and stole at the same time. (Pour out more salt from sin-box into heart-box.) He also buried this in the tent. (Place handkerchief over box again.)

THE WEDGE OF GOLD

Any one who would disobey God and steal a Sunday suit would be apt to steal silver and gold, too.

Achan went out again. This time he found a great, valuable bar of gold. He tucked it under his coat and ran to his tent again, and buried it. (Pour out the rest of salt. Cover heart-box with handkerchief again.)

THE BATTLE OF AI

Near the city of Jericho, as far as —— (a nearby local town) is from our town, was a little village, with a little name. It is spelled with two letters—A-I. Let us all say these two letters together. A-I. That is the way it is pronounced.

Joshua sent a small army of soldiers to capture that town. Soon the soldiers came running back. Some of them never did come back, for they were killed in battle.

Joshua was greatly surprised, for he had sent more than enough to capture all the people in Ai.

THE CURSE IN THE CAMP

Then God told Joshua that the curse was upon the camp of Israel, because someone had disobeyed, and had taken the spoils of the city.

THE TRIBES GATHERED

Joshua called all the tribes together, to find the person who was guilty. All declared they knew nothing about the matter.

Then he came finally to Achan. Joshua said, "Achan, did you disobey and steal, and bring the curse upon us?"

Boys and girls, anybody who would disobey and steal, would also tell lies.

Achan said, "No, Joshua, I didn't. You can search me, for I have no sin in my life." (Carefully turn heart-box upside down, not holding mouth of box toward children. To their surprise, the salt will not come out. Fig. 11.)

Achan thought he had fooled Joshua, by so cleverly hiding the spoils in his tent, and his sin in his heart.

THE CANDLE

Joshua was not satisfied. He continued his search. He appointed other soldiers to search out the camp. With lanterns and torches, they went into every dark tent and looked. (Light candle or hold it up.)

BACK TO ACHAN'S TENT

Soon they came to Achan's tent. (Place handkerchief over box. Fig. 13. With your finger, break open the gummed paper that covers the cut-out hole in the funnel, as at A in Fig. 5. Push the torn paper back, so the salt can be poured out later.)

ACHAN—CAUGHT WITH THE GOODS

The soldiers saw that the ground had been broken under Achan's tent. They dug open the hole and found the robe, the silver and the gold, and brought it to Joshua. (Remove handkerchief.)

They said, "Joshua, Achan is guilty. We have caught him with the goods." (Pour salt out into the glass. Fig. 14.)

So Achan's sin was found out.

THE WAGES OF SIN

Disobedience meant death. Achan was taken out and stoned to death, and his belongings were burned. They rolled his dead body down the hillside and covered it with stones.

WE NEED NOT DIE FOR OUR SINS

(Hold up box with cross on it. This represents Jesus.)

God is not willing that any should perish, but wants all to come to repentance. "God sent not His Son into the world to condemn the world, but that the world through Him might be saved."

Perhaps, boys and girls, you may have sinned, too, by being disobedient or taking what was not yours, or telling a falsehood. If you have, then there are sins hidden in your heart. Let me tell you what to do. The Bible says, "If we confess our sins, He is faithful and just to forgive us our sins and to cleanse us from all unrighteousness."

Here is Jesus represented. (Hold up cross-box.)

And here is your life with sin in it. (Hold up the glass.)

HIDE YOUR SINS IN JESUS

Turn your life over to Jesus, and hide your sins in Him. (Pour the salt from the glass into the cross-box. Fig. 15.)

Jesus said, "Whosoever cometh unto Me, I will in no wise cast out."

The Bible states that, "As far as the east is from the west, so far will He remove our transgressions from us, and will remember them against us no more."

(Turn cross-box upside down, as in Fig. 16.)

If you hide your sins in your heart, you, like Achan, will be caught with the goods; but if you hide them in Jesus, they will be blotted out.

Achan hid his sins from Joshua, and died in his sin.

If you hide your sins in Jesus, you will live for eternity.

124

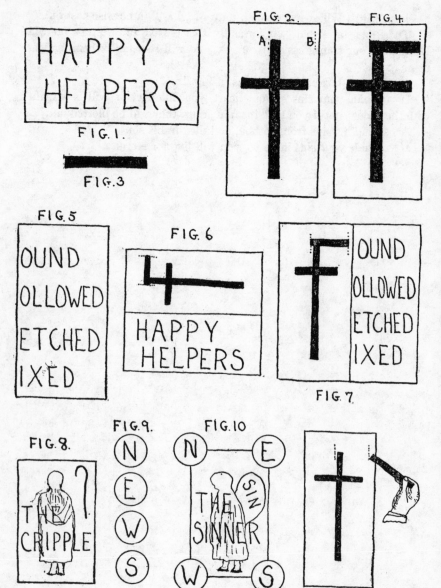

FIG. 1.

FIG. 2.

FIG. 3

FIG. 4.

FIG. 5

FIG. 6

FIG. 7

FIG. 8.

FIG. 9.

FIG. 10

FIG. 11

HAPPY HELPERS

A   B

OUND
OLLOWED
ETCHED
IXED

HAPPY
HELPERS

OUND
OLLOWED
ETCHED
IXED

THE CRIPPLE

N
E
W
S

N   E

THE
SINNER

SIN

W   S

XXII

THE FOUR HAPPY HELPERS

MARK 2:1-5.

MATERIAL NEEDED—

Cardboard.
Crayon or paint.
Paper.
Glue.
Paper-clips.

CONSTRUCTION OF OBJECT—

1. Upon a piece of cardboard, 5 x 8 inches, print HAPPY HELPERS. Fig. 1.

2. Upon another piece of cardboard, the same size, print the figure of a cross. Fig. 2. On this card, cut two slots, with a razor-blade, at points A and B, Fig. 2.

3. Cut a small strip of cardboard. Fig. 3. Colour it the same colour as cross.

4. Slip this strip into slots, to make Fig. 4.

5. With paper and glue, hinge Fig. 1 and Fig. 4 together. Fig. 6.

6. On another piece of cardboard, draw a picture of a crippled man, lying on a pallet. Fig. 8.

7. On other side of this cardboard, draw a man with a pack on his back. Fig. 10.

8. On another piece of cardboard, print letters as in Fig. 5. Hinge this to Fig. 4, making Fig. 7.

9. Cut out four discs and print letters N E W S upon them. Fig. 9.

THE LESSON

The Bible tells us the story of four HAPPY HELPERS. (Show Fig. 6.) They have become very famous, because they helped a crippled man to find Jesus and to be healed.

NAMING THE HAPPY HELPERS

How many happy helpers did I say there were? Yes, four. (Point to 4.) Since they have no names, we should find names for them. (Hold up four discs—N E W S.) Here is one of the helpers, and his initial is N. Suppose we call him NOBODY.

EVERYBODY

Here is the second happy helper. His initial is E. We will name him EVERYBODY. What he did to help the poor crippled man, everybody can do.

WHOSOEVER

Here is the third happy helper. His initial is W. We will give him a Scriptural name. It is found in John 3:16. We will call him WHOSOEVER.

SOMEBODY

Now let us find a name for the fourth happy helper. His initial is S. I would like to call him SOMEBODY.

THESE NAMES REPRESENT ALL OF US

These names include every one of us. NOBODY, EVERYBODY, WHOSO-EVER, SOMEBODY.

There may be a boy or girl here who says, "I am a nobody." You say you can do nothing. You can do as much as this man did.

Another boy or girl may say, "Oh, I am everybody." As you grow older, you will be satisfied to be just yourself, and to carry just your own little corner, for it will be heavy.

Whosoever means all of us.

And somebody—well, we all want to be somebody, don't we?

THE HAPPY HELPERS GET TOGETHER

One day these four happy helpers met on the street. Suddenly Somebody said to Whosoever, "Since we are so happy, let us make someone else happy, too."

They all agreed to this. Then Whosoever said, "Who can we help?"

"Well," said Nobody, to the other three, "of course I am nobody, but I believe if we look around, we can find someone to help."

(Turn the card to position of Fig. 7.)

Down the street they went, and that day those four happy helpers did four great things.

THEY FOUND A CRIPPLED MAN

1. The happy helpers found a crippled beggar, lying on a ragged old pallet, on a street corner, and he was begging for money. At his side on the pallet, was his cane. (Hold up Fig. 8.)

He used this cane to help move himself.

"There," said Whosoever, "we have found a man we can help. You know, this morning I heard about Jesus, a great teacher and healer, and they say He is in our town today. If we can get this crippled man to Jesus, He will heal him and make him strong, and well, and happy. If we make him happy, we will be happy, too."

THEY FOLLOWED THE CRIPPLED MAN

2. Two of the happy helpers watched that poor crippled man, while the other two happy helpers went to find Jesus.

Every time he moved, they moved. *They followed him.*

After some hours the two happy helpers came back. They reported that Jesus was in a house, teaching and healing. They said the house was crowded with people, and many stood outside, listening through the doors and windows.

THEY FETCHED THE CRIPPLED MAN

3. When they got ready to go, Nobody said to Everybody, "You are the biggest, for you are everybody; we will let you carry the crippled man, for you are strong."

Then Whosoever spoke up and said, "No, you are wrong. If we are to be happy helpers, we must all work together. Each of us must have a part and do our share in bringing this man to Jesus. This pallet has four corners, and there are just four of us; so let us each take a corner, and we will all carry him."

This they agreed to do, so they came to the crippled man and said, "We are happy helpers. Our names are NOBODY, EVERYBODY, WHOSOEVER and SOMEBODY. Our initials are N-E-W-S. That spells NEWS. We, the happy helpers, have good news for you. We will take you to Jesus, and He will heal you, so you can throw away your cane and walk without it."

Then each of them took hold of a corner of the pallet, and lifted him up. (With paper-clips, fasten the discs on the corners of the pallet. Fig. 10.)

So the happy helpers found, followed, and fetched the crippled man to Jesus.

Down the street they marched, each holding on to his own corner. If Whosoever had let go, Somebody would then have had to carry two corners.

The curious people watched and many followed, to see where they were going.

Soon they came to the house where Jesus was teaching. All around the house were people, inside and outside.

The happy helpers pushed their way through the crowd, but they were told they could not come in, for there was no room, and especially for beggars.

What do you suppose they did? Well, the house had a flat roof, and oftentimes the people went up on the roof to visit with their friends. The roof was like a front porch, and there were steps leading up to it.

The happy helpers carried the crippled man up these steps, and cut a big hole in the roof, and let the crippled man down through this hole, and there he was, right in front of Jesus.

JESUS FIXED HIM

4. Jesus loved the poor and helpless and sick and needy. He looked with great pity on this crippled man. He stopped His teaching for a moment, and reached forth His tender and kind hand, and put it upon the crippled man's body, and

FIXED HIM

Yes, boys and girls, Jesus healed him. He told him to throw his cane away. That day the man walked home without his cane, and no one had to carry him.

WHO WAS THE HAPPIEST?

I imagine Jesus was very happy that day, as He saw the man walk, and I know the crippled man was happy; but I believe the four happy helpers were happier than all.

THERE ARE CRIPPLES IN OUR TOWN, TOO

Now, children, we have many boys and girls in our town who are worse off than this cripple was. Jesus can help them, too, but we must bring them to Him.

You have some friends, or schoolmates. They may not be crippled, but they have a great burden on them. It is the burden of sin. (Turn Fig. 8 around and show Fig. 10.) Jesus is the only one who can take this burden from them. You have this glad, happy, NEWS for them. Won't you be happy helpers, and go and tell them?

I wish all the Nobodys, and the Everybodys, and the Whosoevers, and the Somebodys would get together and do the four things the four happy helpers did.

You, too, can

> FIND THEM
> FOLLOW THEM
> FETCH THEM
> FIX THEM.

Do you know somebody who does not go to Sunday school? You go out and *find* him. Every day you *follow* him, and invite him to come. Then on Sunday you go to his house and *fetch* him to Sunday school. When he gets there, he will meet Jesus, and Jesus will take that big burden from him, and *fix* him, like He did the poor cripple.

THEY WILL MEET JESUS AT THE FOOT OF THE CROSS

The crippled beggar met Jesus in the house in Capernaum, but when you bring your friends with their sins, they will meet Him at the foot of the Cross.

(Take the strip off the letter F and show the cross. Fig. 11.)

The crippled beggar met Jesus as a teacher and healer, but your friends, when they meet Jesus at the Cross, will meet Him as a SAVIOUR.